Fifty years ago Desmond Hawkins joined the BBC's South & West Region and began what can only be adequately described as a love-affair with the landscapes, the history, the literature and the people of the West Country, and more specifically of central southern England (comprising the counties of Dorset, Wiltshire and Somerset). These have been the subject of his books, TV films, radio documentaries and magazine articles, with Cranborne Chase as a major focal point.

Since his retirement as the BBC's Regional Controller in 1970 Desmond Hawkins has lived in Dorset. A keen conservationist, he was awarded the Silver Medal of the Royal Society for the Protection of Birds in 1959. In 1977 he was elected a Fellow of the Royal Society of Literature.

His other books include *Hardy's Wessex; Hardy, Novelist and Poet; Hardy at Home; Cranborne Chase; Avalon and Sedgemoor; The Grove Diaries;* and a volume of autobiography, *When I Was.*

DORSET BEDSIDE BOOK

A Collection of Prose and Poetry

SELECTED AND INTRODUCED BY
DESMOND HAWKINS

THE DOVECOTE PRESS

To the remembrance of Ralph Wightman (1907-1971)
who, in his day, epitomised Dorset.

First published in 1996 by The Dovecote Press Ltd
Stanbridge, Wimborne, Dorset BH21 4JD

ISBN 1 874336 38 5

Photoset in Sabon by The Typesetting Bureau,
Wimborne, Dorset
Printed and bound by The Baskerville Press
Salisbury, Wiltshire

1 3 5 7 8 6 4 2

CONTENTS

INTRODUCTION

What exactly is a "bedside" book? I think of it as being like a cupboard of toys that children open on a rainy day when they are confined indoors. At the day's end many readers like to have a book at hand when they go to bed, to dip into for a few minutes before settling to sleep; and if it draws its inspiration from the county in which they live, even perhaps in which they were born and bred, so much the better!

Here then is a Dorset miscellany – a celebration of the sights and sounds of the county, its history, its scenery, its people. Some of its qualities it may share with its neighbouring counties, but Dorset is unmistakably Dorset in many ways. It proclaims its identity in the Cerne Giant, the Chesil Beach and the Abbotsbury Swannery, Blue Vinny Cheese, the Cobb at Lyme Regis, the Tolpuddle Martyrs' memorial, the cottage where Thomas Hardy was born, the memories of George III at Weymouth. These and many more provide the quintessential flavours of Dorset that I have endeavoured to convey in my selection.

Dorset is not a large county – exactly the same size as Madeira according to James Dugdale in his *New British Traveller*, 1819 – but its extremely complex geology provides a remarkable variety of landscapes. Visitors, particularly from the wide unchanging horizons of America, frequently express their delight in the way that the passing of only a few miles brings completely fresh scenes. Sandy heath, clay vale, chalk down and limestone ring the changes with marble and sandstone and shale. 'All the best of England in a little space', was Ralph Wightman's claim for his native county; 'and to crown it all', he added, 'we have the sea'.

DESMOND HAWKINS, 1996

I · THE DORSET COAST

The coast can mean many different things to mariners, fishermen, sea birds, day-trippers, bathers and beachcombers, to name a few of those who are drawn to the cliffs, the rocks and the coves where land and ocean meet. As Sir Frederick Treves points out, Dorset has a quite remarkable variety in the composition of its coastline, which accounts for its many changes of mood and style in the space of a few miles.

The statue of George III in Weymouth is a reminder of the town's great days of royal patronage – still so vivid in the pages of Fanny Burney's diary; and when the world of fashion moved elsewhere, the railway brought the new breed of trippers from the workshops of Swindon. Bournemouth comes later in the story, a Victorian utopia conjured out of an empty wilderness by the rising middle-class prosperity. Lyme Regis in its ups and downs has its special devotees and its strong literary associations. Tennyson made a pilgrimage to Lyme to see the famous scene that Jane Austen described in Persuasion. Away from the towns are still the unnoticed coves and little beaches where someone may be landing a few mackerel, to be freshly cooked in the way Ralph Wightman describes.

A Stretch of the Dorset Coast

I doubt if there be around England a more picturesque stretch of coast, for its length, than that which borders the sea from Swanage to Weymouth. Certainly there is no shore which presents so many contrasts and variations in so few pleasant miles. In this sea line are cliffs of jagged rocks, sheer as a bastion wall, as well as green lawns which creep lazily to the water's edge. There are wide, open bays, and fissured sea-echoing chines. There are round coves, inlets reached through arched rocks, level sands, and moaning caves. There are beaches of shingle, of pebbles, of colossal boulders, and of the clay of crumbling banks; precipices of every colour, from the white of chalk to the black of the shale; and walls of stone streaked with tints of yellow, buff or red.

After leaving Swanage the coast is drab and savage, the cliffs erect or scooped out in places by quarries. There is no beach. The rock rampart, cracked by sinister rents, rises from the sea above evil-looking ledges and hollow sea halls. At Dancing Ledge a sheltered bay has been fretted in the cliff. In the place of the beach a flat, acre-wide slab of rock slides into the sea, like the slope in harbours for the hauling up of boats. The sea swirls smoothly over the glacis, as if it were feeling it with blind hands, and then falls off by the far end into a pool of foam. An iron ladder leads down to the ledge, which is a place slippery with death in a rising tide.

Winspit, two miles westward, is a lonely, tragic spot. It is here that a valley comes down to the Channel, to a cleft in the cliffs so narrow as to be like a Titanic hatchet cut. In this gap is a beach of boulders wedged in between high walls. On the strand are a boat and the wreck of another. Just above the creek, where the grass begins, is a cottage in a garden. The place is a solitude. There is ever a moan of the wind in the gap, while from the cottage windows can only be seen the sky and the downs. This harsh place, with the castaway house and the boat in the gorge, may pass for a scene from some drama of the toilers of the deep. It is near here that the *Halsewell*, East Indiaman, was wrecked in 1786, with the loss of 168 lives.

In the museum at Dorchester is an old hour-glass, a sturdy, rugged thing of stout wood and thick green glass. It runs for four hours, and was used to time the watch on the *Halsewell*. When that vessel foundered this hour-glass was washed ashore unhurt, while human beings were mangled beyond recognition on the rocks.

Sir Frederick Treves (Highways & Byways in Dorset, 1906)

Mackerel Picnic

On the way home we stopped on the Chesil Beach at Abbotsbury where the edge of the sea consists of a huge mound of pebbles twenty feet high and eight miles long. On the beach the men of Abbotsbury were fishing. All day they work on farms in the district, but at night they go down to the beach with a long net and a boat. Four of them hold a rope attached to the net, and four row out, throwing out the net as they go. They row round in a semi-circle and land, and then both parties of four begin to haul in the net so that every fish in the semi-circle is taken. On the 20th May they caught about a thousand mackerel in one cast. We borrowed a bucket from them and cooked four mackerel in sea-water on the beach. I have never tasted anything better than hot, fresh fish cooked in sea-water, and eaten with the fingers.

Ralph Wightman (My Homeward Road, 1950)

King George at Weymouth 1798

The loyalty of all this place is excessive; they have dressed out every street with labels of 'God save the King'; all the shops have it over the doors; all the children wear it in their caps – all the labourers in their hats, and all the sailors *in their voices*; for they never approach the house without shouting it aloud – nor see the King, or his shadow, without beginning to huzza, and going on to three cheers.

The bathing machines make it their motto over all their windows; and those bathers that belong to the royal dippers wear it in bandeaux on their bonnets, to go into the sea; and have it again, in large letters, round their waists, to encounter the waves. Flannel dresses, tucked up, and no shoes nor stockings, with bandeaux and girdles, have a most singular appearance; and when first I surveyed these loyal nymphs, it was with some difficulty I kept my features in order.

Nor is this all. Think but of the surprise of his Majesty when, the first time of his bathing, he had no sooner popped his royal head under water than a band of music, concealed in a neighbouring machine, struck up 'God save great George our King.'

One thing, however, was a little unlucky: when the Mayor and burgesses came with the address, they requested leave to kiss hands.

This was graciously accorded; but, the Mayor advancing in a common way, *to take the Queen's hand*, as he might that of any lady mayoress, Colonel Gwynn, who stood by, whispered: 'You must kneel, sir!' He found, however, that he took no notice of this hint, but kissed the Queen's hand erect. As he passed him, in his way back, the Colonel said: 'You should have knelt, sir!' 'Sir,' answered the poor Mayor, 'I cannot.' 'Everybody does, sir.' 'Sir – I have a wooden leg!' Poor man! Such a surprise! And such an excuse as no one could dispute.

Fanny Burney (1789)

Lulworth Cove

West Lulworth is 12 miles W. from Peverel Point. On the coast, at a little distance from the village, is Lulworth Cove, a sort of natural bason, into which the sea flows through a gap in the cliff, wide enough to admit a vessel of 70 or 80 tons burthen. "The rocks around it," observes Dr. Maton, "rise to a great height, particularly those opposite the entrance, which are composed of a hard, calcareous grit. Those nearer to the main sea consist of a shelly lime-stone (similar to that of Peverel Point, and St. Adhelm's Head) and chert; and it is observable, that the strata of these substances on one side of the Cove correspond exactly to those on the other, both in direction and texture. It may be remarked too, that the whole range, quite from Peverel Point, makes the same angle, about forty-five degrees from the horizon, or nearly so, pitching, or dipping, in general, to the north.

The rocks west of the cave have been undermined in a singular manner by the sea, and there are large grotesque caverns, through which it pours with an awful roar. Immense masses seem just ready to drop into the deep, exhibiting marks of some wonderful convulsion: alterations in their aspect daily take place, and the depth and extent of the sea within the Cove, have considerably increased even in the memory of several natives of the village. About these rocks, the razor-bill and puffin lay their eggs. They generally make their appearance towards the middle of May, and migrate before the end of August. The former deposits its eggs on the bare rocks; and even those belonging to different birds are placed contiguous to each other. These eggs are food for the country people, who often run most terrific risks, by trusting themselves at the end of a rope to the strength of only one person above, if whose footing should be insecure, they must both tumble down the precipice together."

James Dugdale (*The New British Traveller, 1819*)

Lyme Regis: The Cobb (1)

An easterly is the most disagreeable wind in Lyme Bay – Lyme Bay being that largest bite from the underside of England's outstretched southwestern leg – and a person of curiosity could at once have deduced several strong probabilities about the pair who began to walk down the quay at Lyme Regis, the small but ancient eponym of the inbite, one incisively sharp and blustery morning in the late March of 1867.

The Cobb has invited what familiarity breeds for at least seven hundred years, and the real Lymers will never see much more to it than a long claw of old grey wall that flexes itself against the sea. In fact, since it lies well apart from the main town, a tiny Piraeus to a microscopic Athens, they seem almost to turn their backs on it. Certainly it has cost them enough in repairs through the centuries to justify a certain resentment. But to a less tax-paying, or more discriminating, eye it is quite simply the most beautiful sea-rampart on the south coast of England. And not only because it is, as the guidebooks say, redolent of seven hundred years of English history, because the ships sailed to meet the Armada from it, because Monmouth landed beside it ... but finally because it is a superb fragment of folk-art.

Primitive yet complex, elephantine but delicate; as full of subtle curves and volumes as a Henry Moore or a Michelangelo; and pure, clean, salt, a paragon of mass. I exaggerate? Perhaps, but I can be put to the test, for the Cobb has changed very little since the year of which I write; though the town of Lyme has, and the test is not fair if you look back towards land.

However, if you had turned northward and landward in 1867, as the man that day did, your prospect would have been harmonious. A picturesque congeries of some dozen or so houses and a small boatyard – in which, arklike on its stocks, sat the thorax of a lugger – huddled at where the Cobb runs back to land. Half a mile to the east lay, across sloping meadows, the thatched and slated roofs of Lyme itself; a town that had its heyday in the Middle Ages and has been declining ever since. To the west sombre grey cliffs, known locally as Ware Cleeves, rose steeply from the shingled beach where Monmouth entered upon his idiocy. Above them and beyond, stepped massively inland, climbed further cliffs masked by dense woods. It is in this aspect that the Cobb seems most a last bulwark – against all that wild eroding coast to the west. There too I can be put to proof. No house lay visibly then or, beyond a brief misery of beach-huts, lies today in that direction.

John Fowles (The French Lieutenant's Woman, 1969)

Lyme Regis: The Cob (2)

The Cob is a mole built in the sea, about two furlongs from the town, and named from the cobble stone of which it is compiled. There is not any one like it in the world: for though it is an immense mass of stone, of the shape of a demilune, with a bar in the middle of the concave, no one stone that lies there was ever touched with a tool or is bedded in any sort of cement; but all, being pebbles of the sea, are piled up and hold by their bearings only, and the surge plays in and out through the interstices of the stone in a wonderful manner. That this must often decay is certain; for the best-cemented square stone will scarce hold against the surge. But there is warning enough to alarm the town to repair and thereby to prevent any great ruin of it; for sometimes a swamp will appear in the flat top where they walk; and, when that is perceived, they go to work and take down all that part, and build it up from the bottom; and nothing less will prevent the downfall of much more, sooner or later, as the seas rage more or less against it. And it may happen that some new foundation stones are to be laid. Those are the largest sort that can be got; and they search them out upon the coast, and mounting them upon casks chained together, with but one man mounted upon them, he with the help of a pole conducts it to the place where it is to lie and then, striking out an iron pin, away go the casks and the stone falls in its place. The vessels of burthen are laden and unladen by horses, turning and returning upon the sand between the Cob and the town: and they have no drivers, but are charged with bales (for instance) at the warehouse, and away they trot to the ship side and stand fair, sometimes above the belly in water, for the tackle to discharge them; and then they gallop back to the warehouse for more; and so they perform the tide's work and know, by the flood, when their labour is at an end. I must own, I could scarce have believed this description if I had not seen the place and the poor horses at work: and I cannot but wonder that our topographers have taken no more notice than they have done of it.

Roger North (The Lives of the Norths, 1890)

The Musgroves Visit Lyme Regis

After securing accommodations, and ordering a dinner at one of the inns, the next thing to be done was unquestionably to walk directly down to the sea. They were come too late in the year for any amusement or variety which Lyme, as a public place, might offer. The rooms were shut up, the lodgers almost all gone, scarcely any family but of the residents left; and as there is nothing to admire in the buildings themselves, the remarkable situation of the town, the principal street almost hurrying into the water, the walk of the Cobb (skirting round the pleasant little bay, which, in the season, is animated with bathing machines and company), the Cobb itself, its old wonders and new improvements, with the very beautiful line of cliffs stretching out to the east of the town, are what the stranger's eye will seek; and a very strange stranger it must be who does not see charms in the immediate environs of Lyme to make him wish to know it better. The scenes in its neighbourhood – Charmouth, with its high grounds and extensive sweeps of country, and still more its sweet, retired bay, backed by dark cliffs, where fragments of low rock among the sands make it the happiest spot for watching the flow of the tide, for sitting in unwearied contemplation; the woody varieties of the cheerful village of Up Lyme; and, above all, Pinny, with its green chasms between romantic rocks, where the scattered forest trees and orchards of luxuriant growth declare that many a generation must have passed away since the first partial falling of the cliff prepared the ground for such a state, where a scene so wonderful and so lovely is exhibited as may more than equal any of the resembling scenes of the far-famed Isle of Wight – these places must be visited, and visited again, to make the worth of Lyme understood.

Next day they again visited the Cobb, where Louisa Musgrove met with an accident which at first appeared to have cost her her life.

There was too much wind to make the high part of the new Cobb pleasant for the ladies, and they agreed to get down the steps to the lower; and all were contented to pass quietly and carefully down the steep flight, excepting Louisa: she must be jumped down them by Captain Wentworth. In all their walks he had had to jump her from the stiles; the sensation was delightful to her. The hardness of the pavement for her feet made him less willing upon the present occasion; he did it however. She was safely down, and instantly to show her enjoyment, ran up the steps to be jumped down again. He advised her against it, thought the jar too great; but no, he reasoned and talked in vain; she smiled and said, 'I am determined I will.' He put out his hands, she was too precipitate by half a second; she fell on the pavement on the lower Cobb, and was taken up lifeless!

There was no wound, no blood, no visible bruise; but her eyes were closed, she breathed not, her face was like death. The horror of that moment to all who stood around!

Captain Wentworth, who had caught her up, knelt with her in his arms, looking on her with a face as pallid as her own, in an agony of silence.

Jane Austen (Persuasion, 1818)

Low Water in Lyme Regis

About the year 1750 the town was, generally speaking, in a very low state. Some might think this has been exaggerated, when it appears there was no want felt. However, nearly the whole population was engaged in the manufacture of serges, which was then carried on by a few individuals of respectability, and at that time conducted in a manner quite different from that of the present day, as men took home work which they wove at their own houses. These men were poor; there was little shipping; no influx of strangers, and very few respectable inhabitants. Houses were of little value; purchasers could scarcely be procured on any terms, and some were literally given away, while others are known to have been offered, but refused! The lower street had large high buildings, some of which projected at each story, which had been the abode in the former century of rich families, but from the effects of time and neglect of the poorer occupiers, were in a state of extreme decay. The population had dwindled to less than a thousand inhabitants, so that a great many houses remained unoccupied, and were so neglected that it is an incontestable fact that no one could walk with safety in the streets during a high wind, which frequently blew down parts of the most tottering buildings.

During the summer months a few invalids occasionally came to enjoy the sea air; but as machines were unknown, anyone wishing to court the embraces of Neptune was obliged to undress on the beach: the accommodations in other respects were equally bad. The inn-keeper first procured a bathing-machine for the accommodation of travellers, who were enabled to take a dip in a comfortable manner, before proceeding on their journey. It is a curious fact that he placed it at the mouth of the river, where it remained for several years. Bathing soon became a favourite, or rather fashionable prescription, with medical practitioners. Many a lovely creature, whose tender frame was shaken by an insidious malady beyond hope of cure, shivered at each plunge; and those in robust health were daily seen in numbers playing mermaids and tritons. Nearly every visitor to the coast was a bather; now, (1833,) comparatively few take the cold bath, excepting as a luxury. The warm baths are in greater request.

Housekeepers near the sea began to fit up two or three front rooms in a homely manner, which is the first indication at Lyme of the lodg-ing-house system, now so generally pursued on the whole line of the coast: they met with encouragement, others were procured, and it soon happened, as it is somewhere expressed, that the invalids who came in search of health "found the goddess propitious to their prayers, and returning to pay their vows, brought beauty and elegance in their train." An agreeable society was formed in the summer months. Some families professed themselves partial to Lyme; and a few gentlemen, animated by public spirit, caused the Assembly rooms to be erected, which, conducted on the most liberal plan of any in England, may be considered to have rescued the town from impending ruin. Before that time the respectable inhabitants and visitors occasionally met to dance in the alcove on the walk.

George Roberts (History and Antiquities of Lyme Regis, 1834)

Bournemouth in 1847

Ally [her daughter, Alethea], is at Bourn Mouth and she likes the place very much, so quiet and good bathing and Poole, their post town, so primitive.

Lady Stanley of Alderley (1847)

Twentieth Century Bournemouth

The sea is only one of the things about Bournemouth, and one of the least interesting. Bathing is safe. Sands are firm and sprinkled in places with shingle and in others with children. There are lines of bathing huts, bungalows and tents and deck chairs municipally owned, mostly above that long high water mark which hardly changes at all, for the tide at Bournemouth always seems to be high. The sea to Bourne-mouth is incidental, like the bathroom leading out of a grand hotel suite: something which is there because it ought to be, and used for hygienic reasons. Deep in a chine with its scent of resin and tap of palm leaves and plash of streamlets and moan of overhanging pine, an occasional whiff of ozone reminds us of the sea. But Bournemouth is mainly a residential town by the sea, not a seaside town full in summer only.

The inland suburbs of Bournemouth are like any other suburbs, indistinguishable from Wembley or the Great West Road. And they stretch for miles, leaving here and there a barren patch of pylon-bisected heath. The main shopping streets have the usual ugly lengths of flashy chromium, though a pretty, early-Victorian stucco thorough-fare survives called the Arcade. The public buildings are less blatant and alien looking than the latest blocks of flats and hotels. But the beauty of Bournemouth consists in three things, her layout, her larger villas and her churches. All of these are Victorian.

Earliest Bournemouth is on the western and Branksome side of the Bourne which runs into the sea by the Pavilion. It consists of a few villas built by Mr Lewis Tregonwell, whose name survives in a terrace and a road and whose house was part of the Exeter Hotel. He started building in 1810. In 1836 a local landlord, Sir George Tapps of Wes-tover and Hinton Admiral, built on the eastern bank of the stream.

Adding Gervis to his name, he went on building and called in Benjamin Ferrey, the Gothic church architect and friend of Pugin, to lay out his estate. Thus Gervis Place arose with its stucco Tudor-style villas. Tudor or Italian, the villas were varied, well spaced in the setting, roads were broad and planted with trees, but everything had to wind. Nothing was to be regular. That is why there is no formal promenade in Bournemouth and why there have always been so many foot-paths and curving roads in the older and finer parts of the town. The place was carefully planned from its beginnings on the principle that nature abhors a straight line, the picturesque school of Georgian gardening surviving into Victorian times.

This sense that Bournemouth is a garden with houses in it survived the century. The name Tapps-Gervis increased to Tapps-Gervis-Meyrick, hence Meyrick Avenue, Meyrick Park, Meyrick Road. And if you are not sure of the owner of the road, you may often guess its date from its name – Adelaide, Alma, Gladstone. They are hidden behind trees and flowering shrubs, down lengths of gravel bordered with rhododendron, these Victorian villas. Some are hotels, some are now government offices. They reflect every phase of leisured Victorian and Edwardian life – here a hint of Madeira, there an Elizabethan cottage, then an Italian villa like the Royal Bath Hotel. All these are in stucco and not later than the 'seventies'. Then brick came in and we have 'Flemish style' buildings, with gables and white wood balconies and leaded panes, of which J.D. Sedding's Vicarage of St Clements and big house at the top of Boscombe Chine, called The Knole, are beautiful, satisfying examples. They look stately and practical. Later, a brilliant local architect, Sidney Tugwell, designed villas in the new art style with tiny windows fluttering cheerful chintz, low-pitched roofs of local stone and broad eaves – wholesome and simple buildings like home-made cakes. He had his imitators. And each of these strongly individual Victorian houses, not content with its garden-like road, Knyveton Road, Manor Road, Alum Chine or further inland around Meyrick Park, has, or once had, a beautiful garden of its own. So that the real Bournemouth is all pines and pines and pines and flowering shrubs, lawns, begonias, azaleas, bird-song, dance tunes, the plung of the racket and creak of the basket chair.

Lastly the churches have the colour and clearness of the town. I doubt if any place in Britain has finer modern churches than

Bournemouth and, what is more, they are all open and all alive. I visited fourteen of them on one week-day and found them all clean and cared for and in most of them people at prayer. Excluding Parkstone with its beautiful St Peter's and the lovely Basilica of St Osmund I thought the finest Bournemouth church was St Stephen's in the centre of the town – designed by J.L. Pearson. It is worth travelling 200 miles and being sick in the coach to have seen the inside of this many-vistaed church, all in clean cream-coloured stone, with arch cutting arch, a lofty hall of stone vaulting providing view after view as you walk round it, each lovelier than the next and worthy of a vast cathedral.

Away in the suburbs there is much that is beautiful, J.D. Sedding's famous church of St Clement, scholarly and West-country looking in stone; Sir Giles Gilbert Scott's little Roman Catholic Church of the Annunciation, a brilliantly original design in brick, his first work after Liverpool Cathedral; St Francis' church by J. Harold Gibbons on a new building estate, white, Italianate and vast. As the day drew to an end I entered a red-brick church in a hard red-brick shopping street at the back of Boscombe. St Mary's Boscombe, built about 1920. Here, out of the noise of the street, was a white, cool and spacious interior, friendly, beautiful, with golden screens and gold and blue east windows, gaily painted roofs and wide and high West-country arches. Clean and white and cheerful, the perfect seaside church. That last experience seemed to typify Bournemouth. You arrive tired from a long journey, you first see only the car parks, buses and jazzy blocks of flats and hotels. You turn into a side road and all is colour, light and life.

John Betjeman (First and Last Loves, 1952)

Swindon by the Sea

At Whitsuntide the first outings are generally held. Then many of the workmen – those who can afford it, who have no large gardens to care for, and who are exempt from other business and anxieties – begin to make short week-end trips by the trains. The privilege of a quarter-fare for travel, granted by the railway companies to their employees, is valued and appreciated, and widely patronised. By means of this very many have trips and become acquainted with the world who otherwise would be unable to do so.

When the men come back to work after the Whitsuntide holidays they usually find the official noticeboard in the shed covered with posters containing the preliminary announcements of the annual Trip, and, very soon, on the plates of the forges and walls, and even outside in the town, the words 'Roll on, Trip,' or 'Five weeks to Trip,' may be seen scrawled in big letters. As the time for the holiday draws near the spirits of the workmen – especially of the younger ones, who have no domestic responsibilities – rise considerably. Whichever way one turns he is greeted with the question – often asked in a jocular sense – 'Wher' gwain Trip?' the reply to which usually is – 'Same old place,' or 'Up in the smowk;' i.e. to London, or 'Swindon by the Sea.' By the last-named place Weymouth is intended. That is a favourite haunt of the poorer workmen who have large families, and it is especially popular with the day trippers.

Every year five or six thousand are conveyed to the Dorsetshire watering-place, the majority of whom return the same evening. Given fine weather an enjoyable day will be spent about the sands and upon the water, but if it happens to rain the outing will prove a wretched fiasco. Sometimes the trippers have left home in fine weather and found a deluge of rain setting in when they arrived at the seaside town. Under such circumstances they were obliged to stay in the trains all day for shelter, or implore the officials to send them home again before the stipulated time.

Alfred Williams (Life in a Railway Factory, 1915)

Poole Quay

Always for work, this old chipped wharf.
Poole wears water like a scarf
wrapped tightly round its throat,
hugging coal and crane, the summer boat,
ferry, and all the habitually transient
against the quay's skin. Each vessel implements
the desire of history to be recalled: -
this stone wall has long excelled
at meeting the tide's volition,
countering it, turning it to tradition.

They would have understood, the old Poole men,
they would have smiled to watch us when
we look down the deeps of water at our feet,
knowing as we do that we meet
by implication every country's shore
that touches it, see in the port a whore
trading their harsh integrity
for the cold demanding bargain of the sea.

Always on the edge of tidescape,
clasped by Arne, Branksey and the steeps
of Purbeck against the shout of storm,
turning a back on farms for a life informed
by Ocean's huge uncertainties,
by distances' higher possibilities.

Two stars suddenly shine, green, red,
and now the water is inhabited.
We encounter another world, exchanging one
with Dorset islands for the harbour of St. John.
Then, looking back, the ancient quay
becomes a haunted place; next, the fray
of ocean, tide and current: – will
enough to take us to their task. Ill
betide the man who looks behind him now . . .
Poole astern – towards Newfoundland the prow!

Sean Street (This True Making, 1992)

Moonfleet Bay

Our village lies near the centre of Moonfleet Bay, a great bight twenty
miles across, and a death-trap to up-channel sailors in a south-westerly
gale. For with that wind blowing strong from south, if you cannot
double the *Snout*, you must most surely come ashore; and many a good
ship failing to round that point has beat up and down the bay all day,
but come to beach in the evening. And once on the beach, the sea has
little mercy, for the water is deep right in, and the waves curl over full
on the pebbles with a weight no timbers can withstand. Then if poor

fellows try to save themselves, there is a deadly *under-tow* or rush back of the water, which sucks them off their legs, and carries them again under the thundering waves. It is that back-suck of the pebbles that you may hear from miles inland, even at Dorchester, on still nights long after the winds that caused it have sunk, and which makes people turn in their beds, and thank God they are not fighting with the sea on Moonfleet Beach.

John Meade Falkner (Moonfleet, 1898)

2 · SMUGGLERS AND POACHERS

The southern coastal counties are inclined to cherish the remembered exploits of smugglers with an indulgent fondness, and Dorset is no exception. They have become a romantic element in folk history. The only victim they robbed was the tax-gatherer, who has never inspired much public sympathy.

Natural allies of the smugglers were the poachers, with their expertise in unobtrusive movement through the countryside and a talent for hiding what they had recently acquired. The landing of contraband was only the first step: it had to be transported to the towns and cities.

What is not remembered quite so cordially is the killing or maiming of those who were caught up in some affray. 'The Battle of Mudeford' and 'The Affray in Cranborne Chase' add their darker tones to the more light-hearted picture.

Smuggling in Dorset

During the eighteenth and early nineteenth centuries many of the inhabitants of south coast towns and villages were deeply involved in the smuggling trade. In Dorset, from Branksome Chine on the east to Lyme Regis on the west, almost every harbour, beach or gap in the cliffs was a smugglers' haunt. Tea, tobacco, lace, silks and brandy formed the bulk of the cargoes. High import duties were imposed upon all these articles, and they were sufficiently valuable to make the risk-taking worth while. They were also easily portable when they had to be carried inland and could obtain a ready sale in any district.

When wages were low, many labourers would willingly come down to the shore on a dark night to earn half-a-crown by tub carrying, and the leaders of the gangs knew exactly how to provide themselves with the men they needed.

In 1736 a Smuggling Act was passed which imposed severe penalties upon those who were engaged in this illicit trade. 'Riding Officers' were placed at strategic points along the coast and efforts were made to prevent their becoming intimate with the local people. They were not allowed to marry girls from the neighbourhood in which they worked and they lived in special quarters. But they were paid only £20 a year and out of this they had to keep three horses and a man to help them. As a result they were easily corruptible and the smugglers usually knew exactly how to 'square' them. In 1779, 1784 and 1805 the Smuggling Act was made more severe by Parliament, but the problem of how to cope with the evil still remained unsolved. Soldiers stationed near the coast could be called to aid the officers and excisemen, but nearly everybody had a sneaking sympathy with the traders and few were above receiving a keg of brandy or a pound of tobacco as the price of silence. It was not until the coastguards were organised in 1831 that the smugglers found effective opposition and, with the abolition of many of the duties during the next twenty years, the old gangs disappeared.

Traditions of these old days are many and various. At Kinson the church tower was used as a hiding place for brandy kegs, which were hauled up by rope. Traces of this can still be seen in the worn condition of the coping stones. Some say a tombstone at the church door was movable, to enable the contraband goods to be hidden there, and that a parish hearse called a Shillibeer used often to be requisitioned, 'not for dead bodies either.' The whole neighbourhood was engaged in these pursuits, including the well-known families of Fryers and Gullivers. A track was known to exist from Branksome Chine to Kinson, across the bleak moorland, a part of which leading through the Talbot Woods was known as 'Pugs Hole.' The old mud walled house at East Howe, 'Howe Lodge,' where the Gullivers lived, was said to have a subterranean passage leading into its large cellars where there was a large open chimney with a small door in it some ten feet up. This door gave access to a chamber above which had no other outlet and which was used as a secret hiding place from 'the Law.'

Dorset Up Along and Down Along, 1935

Dorset Smugglers

... The most sturdy, and not the least respectable of the inhabitants of the surrounding villages, Knighton, Warmwell, Woodsford, Tincleton, were all, on occasion, smugglers. They would work in the fields through a long summer's day; start, at dusk, for the cliffs of Ringsted or Whitenose, eight or nine miles off; meet, as arranged, the little craft which ran into a creek laden with illicit spirits, and sometimes, after a smart brush with the "Government folk," more often quite un-molested, would return by dawn of day, carrying each of them a keg or two of brandy on his back, and then go to work as if nothing had happened, and as if they had been sleeping peacefully in their beds all night. Many a story of such brushes or of hair-breadth escapes have I heard, when a boy, from one of these smugglers, George Treviss, who had long been transformed into an underkeeper. "Did you ever," I asked him one day, in strict confidence, "cut about or kill any of the Government folk?" "No," was the reply, "but I have helped tie 'em to a post often."

R. Bosworth Smith (Bird Life and Bird Lore, 1909)

The Smugglers of Christchurch

The shore of the noble promontory, *Hengistbury Head*, at the southern extremity of the united Avon and Stour rivers, was a spot frequently chosen as a landing place for the contraband goods. Of this grand feature of the coast, our elevated school-room, which runs over the chancel of the church, commanded a perfect view; and, with the assistance of a tolerable glass, enabled us to distinguish every moving object, on the declivity of *Hengistbury Head*. It is doubtless in the recollection of many of the ancient inhabitants of Christchurch, that this descent often presented a living picture of a most singular character. I have myself, more than once, seen a procession of twenty or thirty waggons, loaded with kegs of spirits; an armed man sitting at the front and tail of each; and surrounded by a troop of two or three hundred horsemen, every one carrying on his enormous saddle, from two to four tubs of spirits; winding deliberately, and with the most picturesque and imposing effect, along the skirts of *Hengistbury Head*, in their way towards the wild country to the north-west of Christchurch, the point of their separation. The revenue troop, who had always intelligence of the run, were, it is true, present on the occasion; but with no other views and intentions, than those of perfect peace. A flood of homely jokes were poured upon them by the passing ruffians; but, these were always accompanied by a present of kegs, greater or less, according to the quantity of the smuggled goods; a voluntary toll received, as it was conferred, in perfect good humour, and with mutual satisfaction.

Richard Warner (Literary Recollections, 1830)

The Signal to the Smugglers

From hostile shores returning, glad I look
On native scenes again, and first salute
Thee, Burton[1], and thy lofty cliff, where oft
The nightly blaze is kindled; further seen
Than erst was that love-tended cresset, hung
Beside the Hellespont: yet not like that
Inviting to the hospitable arms
Of Beauty and Youth, but lighted up, the sign
Of danger, and of ambush'd foes to warn
The stealth-approaching Vessel, homeward bound
From Havre or the Norman isles, with freight
Of wines and hotter drinks, the trash of France,
Forbidden merchandize. Such fraud to quell
Many a light skiff and well-appointed sloop
Lies hovering near the coast, or hid behind
Some curved promontory, in hope to seize
These contraband: vain hope! on that high shore
Station'd, th' associates of their lawless trade
Keep watch, and to their fellows off at sea
Give the known signal; they with fearful haste
Observant, put about the ship, and plunge

[1] Burton Bradstock

Into concealing darkness. As a fox,
That from the cry of hounds and hunters' din
Runs crafty down the wind, and steals away
Forth from his cover, hopeful so t' elude
The not yet following pack, – if chance the shout
Of eager or unpractised boy betray
His meditated flight, back he retires
To shelter him in the thick wood: so these
Retiring, ply to south, and shun the land
Too perilous to approach: and oft at sea
Secure (or ever nigh the guarded coast
They venture) to the trackless deep they trust
Their forfeitable cargo, rundlets small,
Together link'd upon their cable's length,
And to the shelving bottom sunk and fixt
By stony weights; till happier hour arrive
To land it on the vacant beach unrisk'd.

William Crowe (Lewesdon Hill, 1788)

The Battle of Mudeford

Along the beach just before Mudeford the roofs of two strangely-shaped houses can be glimpsed. The circular roof belongs to 'Gundimore', a weird residence built by William Stuart Rose, Member of Parliament for Christchurch in the 1790s. He was a poet and traveller who had fallen in love with Persian tents, and he called this permanent version of his beloved shelter after a poem full of Eastern romance which he himself had written.

Further along the promenade at Mudeford Quay car-park is the site of the bloody Battle of Mudeford which took place in 1784, for the beach that preceded the car park was an ideal landing-spot.

In July, 1784, the sloop-of-war H.M.S. *Orestes* had taken up station in the Solent, mainly as a result of many requests to the Board of Customs. On 14th July she was cruising off Yarmouth, Isle of Wight, on watch for smugglers' ships, when a cutter approached which informed her captain that two smuggling luggers, commanded by William May and William Parrott, were due off the mouth of Christchurch Harbour at Mudeford, and that they were loaded with a huge double cargo of tea and brandy bought in the Channel Islands. By the time *Orestes* had arrived off Beerpan Rocks at Hengistbury Head, with her escort of two Revenue cutters, it was six in the morning and the luggers were already anchored a few yards out from the beach.

Through his telescope, the commander of *Orestes*, Captain Ellis, R.N., could see the smugglers ferrying in casks and packets by rowing-boat from Mudeford, and that, as far as he could judge, about 300 people, ships' crews and residents from Mudeford, Stanpit and even Christchurch itself, were as busy as ants helping to bring on shore the huge illicit cargo and load it into well over fifty wagons drawn by nearly 300 horses.

On seeing the little flotilla of King's ships bearing towards the beach, the smugglers on board the luggers ran their ships as far up the shingle as they could and then started stripping them of sails, spars and all other portable equipment. Captain Ellis snapped his telescope shut and immediately ordered away a cutting-out expedition in six ships' boats with fully armed crews. He was determined to destroy the smugglers' luggers even if it was too late to seize their cargo, for the wagons were now moving off. In command of the cutting-out operation was the sailing-master of *Orestes*, William Allen.

As his six boats rowed up to the sterns of the luggers, Mr. Allen stood up in the sternsheets and loudly called on the smugglers still on board to surrender in the name of the King. It was a brave action, but at the same time foolhardy, for the smugglers' reaction was predictable: a tremendous volley of small-arms fire came from the ships, the beach, and from a breastwork the smugglers had scraped up in the sand-dunes for just such a purpose.

Nothing daunted, the King's men came on in, beached their boats, and flinging themselves into cover, immediately returned the enemy's fire. Seeing them land, the smugglers withdrew to the Haven House Inn and its stables, from the windows and doors of which they kept a constant and well-directed fire. Meanwhile, the King's men were boarding the luggers, making sure they had no more smugglers aboard, and making them their own.

When they had done this, they were able to count the cost, and it was high: many sailors had suffered wounds, and, worst of all, Mr. Allen himself, a young man of only twenty-five, had been mortally struck. His first wound had been from a musket-ball in the thigh, but a second had pierced his right side, gone through his liver, and then penetrated his stomach.

When Captain Ellis saw his cutting-out expedition held down by the smugglers' small-arms fire, he decided it was time to use his large arms. Balls from his cannon hit the tower of the Priory Church at Christchurch, so it was said, and a chain-shot wrapped itself round one of the tall chimneys of the Haven House Inn, afterwards kept for a while as a relic by the landlord.

The Battle of Mudeford is supposed to have lasted, on and off, from six in the morning until nine o'clock at night. The smugglers fought ferociously, doing their traditional job of keeping off the King's men while the contraband was removed. The double cargo they had saved from the King's men was enormous: 120,000 gallons of spirits and between thirty and forty tons of tea!

All the Customs and Naval forces took away were the two luggers and their boats, many wounded sailors, and the corpse of William Allen. He was buried at Cowes with full Naval honours, the escort being the ship's company of all the King's vessels in the engagement, the Officers acting as pall-bearers, and the cortege being led by *Orestes*' marines, marching with arms reversed. Many people at the funeral wept openly, for William Allen had been a fine officer, loved and respected by all who knew him.

At the inquest a verdict was brought in of 'Wilful murder against a person or persons unknown, but that William May and William Parrott, the two reputed masters of the smuggling vessels, were aiding, abetting, assisting and comforting the said murderer or murderers'. The hunt for the killers was on, and at the end of the month a notice appeared in the *Salisbury Journal* offering the very large reward of £200 for information leading to their arrest. In February of the following year Henry Voss, George Coombes and Jonathan Edwards were charged at Winchester Assizes with being implicated in the murder, but as William Allen had died actually on the tide-line, the trial would have to take place in the High Court of Admiralty in London.

The two captains, May and Parrott, were also implicated but they escaped the long arm of the law. The evidence for the prosecution showed how Parrott had fired a musket or blunderbuss from the inn at the Officers' boats and that May had done the same, but it could not be *proved* whether he had fired before or after the King's men had fired at him. The evidence showed that the smugglers had a whole arsenal of weapons, and that they must have had free run of the inn, for they fired from bedroom windows as well as downstairs windows and doors.

The upshot of the trial was that Voss and Edwards were acquitted of both felony and murder, but Coombes was convicted on both counts. His jailers were ordered 'to convey under safe custody the said George Coombes unto the gallows set and placed in the public shame in the River of Thames within the flush of the sea and water and jurisdiction of our Admiralty before the bank called Wapping on Monday the 23rd day of January, there to hang by the neck until he shall be dead according to the maritime customs observed .... And that you are immediately after the execution to take the body of the said George Coombes to be hung in chains at some conspicuous place on the coast of Kent or Essex .... Given under the Great Seal of the High Court of Admiralty.' The Court also gave orders that the body was to be dissected and anatomized.

So on the morning of his execution George Coombes was led out from Newgate Gaol by the Admiralty's Officers, the leader of whom carried their unique mace which was in the form of a silver oar. Coombes' behaviour was exemplary, and after he was dead the orders were changed. His body was brought back to Mudeford and hung in an iron cage from a gibbet on Haven Point, because the crime for which he had died had been committed in that place.

But he did not hang there long: his smuggling mates cut him down and he was given secret Christian burial by a sympathetic parson. The Battle of Mudeford had resulted in death and a huge cargo lost to the Revenue forces, but only one smuggler paid the price: the others implicated had melted away into the mists of Christchurch Harbour.

Geoffrey Morley (Smuggling in Hampshire and Dorset, 1983)

Contraband at Higher Bockhampton

While superintending the church music from 1801 onwards to about 1805, my grandfather used to do a little in smuggling, his house being a lonely one, none of the others in Higher Bockhampton being then built, or only one other. He sometimes had as many as eight 'tubs' in a dark closet (afterwards destroyed in altering staircase) each tub containing 4 gallons. The spirits often smelt all over the house, being proof, & had to be lowered for drinking. The tubs, or little elongated barrels, were of thin staves with wooden hoops: I remember one of them which had been turned into a bucket by knocking out one head, & putting a handle. They were brought at night by men on horseback, 'slung,' or in carts. A whiplash across the window pane would awake my grandfather at 2 or 3 in the morning, & he would dress & go down. Not a soul was there, but a heap of tubs loomed up in front of the door. He would set to work & stow them away in the dark closet aforesaid, & nothing more would happen till dusk the following evening, when groups of dark long-bearded fellows would arrive, & carry off the tubs in two & fours slung over their shoulders. The smugglers grew so bold at last that they would come by day, & my grandmother insisted to her husband that he should stop receiving the tubs, which he did about 1805, though not till at a christening of one of their children they 'had a washing pan of pale brandy' left them by the smugglers to make merry with. Moreover the smugglers could not be got to leave off depositing the tubs for some while, but they did so when a second house was built about 100 yards off.

Many years later, indeed, I think in my mother's time, a large woman used to call, & ask if any of 'it' was wanted cheap. Her hugeness was caused by her having bullocks' bladders slung round her hips, in which she carried the spirits. She was known as 'Mother Rogers'.

Thomas Hardy (1840-1928) Personal notebook

An Affray in Cranborne Chase

On the night of the 16th of December 1780, a very severe battle was fought between the keepers and deer-stealers on Chettle Common, in Burseystool Walk. A gang of these deer-stealers assembled at Pimperne, and were headed by a Serjeant of Dragoons, a native of Pimperne, and then quartered at Blandford, and whose name was Blandford. They came in the night in disguise, armed with deadly offensive weapons called swindgels, resembling flails to thresh corn. They attacked the keepers, who were nearly equal in number, but had no weapons but sticks and short hangers. The first blow that was struck was by the leader of the gang, which broke a knee-cap of the stoutest man in the Chase, who has been lame ever since. Another keeper received a blow from a swindgel, which broke three ribs, and was the cause of his death some time after. The remaining keepers closed in upon their opponents with their hangers, and one of the Dragoon's hands was severed from the arm, just above the wrist, and fell on the ground; the others were also dreadfully cut, and wounded, and obliged to surrender. Blandford's arm was tightly bound with a list garter to prevent its bleeding, and he was carried to the Lodge, where I saw him the next day, and his hand in the window. Peter Beckford, Esq. who was at that time Ranger of the Walk, came early in the morning and brought Mr Dansey, a very eminent surgeon, with him, who dressed the wound. Two young Officers came also in the course of the day to see him. As soon as he was well enough to be removed, he was committed, with his companions, to Dorchester gaol. The hand was buried in Pimperne church-yard, and, as reported, with the honours of war. Several of these offenders were labourers, daily employed by Mr Beckford, and had, the preceding day, dined in his servants' hall, and from thence went to join a confederacy to rob their master. They were all tried by Sir Richard Perryn at the Dorchester assizes, found guilty, and condemned to be transported for seven years; but, in consideration of their great suffering from their wounds in prison, the humane Judge commuted the punishment to confinement in gaol for an indefinite term. The soldier was not dismissed from His Majesty's service, but suffered to retire upon halfpay, or pension; and set up a shop in London, which he denoted a Game-factor's, and dispersed hand-bills at all the public passages, and at all the public places, in order to get customers, one of which he himself put into my hand in the arch-way leading into Lincoln's Inn Square. I immediately recognized him, as he did me; and he said, that if I would deal with him, he would use me well, for he had, in times past, had many hares and pheasants of mine; and had the assurance to ask me if I did not think it a good breeding-season for game. Whether he is living now, I know not; but I know that the person who cut off his hand is alive and well.

William Chafin (Anecdotes of Cranborne Chase, 1818)

The Gamekeeper's Dilemma

*In 1719 it was the duty of John Stainer, gamekeeper, to despatch bas-
kets of game to the London address of his employer, John Eliot, who
owned the manor of Ashmore in Cranborne Chase. Poor Stainer, so far
from being the petty tyrant that gamekeepers were often thought to be,
was unable to stem the incursions of local gentry and sporting parsons
like the Rev William Chafin – as he tried to explain in a letter to Mr
Eliot of 8 November, 1791:*

Sir I send you these few Laines to let you no why I sent no Game last
wick it is not for want of Baskets now but it is for want of game and
that is of moor concequances as I said before game is got very scars on
the manner of Ashmore att presents and weel it may for you have but
one game keeper but you have a great many keelers Sir and most of
them are what they call Parsons thare is my ould frind Mr Chafing
with two or three more with him all with Dubble Barel Guns What
thay plese thay kill Cox ore hens makes [no] Defferances to them and
there is a new Gentleman come to Weast Lodge and very seldem without 2 ore 3 with him all with Dubble Barrell guns where thay plese and
what thay plese.

John Stainer (Letter to John Eliot, 1791)

3 · PORTLAND AND PURBECK

Nowhere does Dorset display its individual character more vividly than in its two 'Isles', Purbeck and Portland, thrusting out into the sea and almost surrounded by it. Steep-sided, rock-faced to the mariner in distress, Portland was aptly described by Thomas Hardy as 'the Gibraltar of Wessex'. The cliffs of Purbeck have a like wildness of nature but the heart of the Isle softens to its foreshore with the great harbour of Poole and the low heathland still surviving between Corfe and Wareham.

What unites the two Isles is that, to borrow a phrase of Kipling's, they are 'sisters under the skin'. Their geological endowment, their wealth of the finest building-stone, is what has written their history. It is not the farmers nor the fishermen who have been the definitive characters here, but the men of the quarries, who dug St Paul's and the streets of London out of their soil.

Purbeck marble and Portland stone are some of the very best building material to be found throughout the length and breadth of the country – and the stone for many of London's most famous buildings was hewn from Portland quarries. Both in Purbeck and in Portland rights and privileges of the quarryman are of ancient origin, and interesting survivals of old customs remain to the present day.

On Shrove Tuesday the Ancient Company of Marblers hold their court at Corfe Castle. The meeting is announced by ringing the church bell. Apprentices are then admitted to the company, but not before they reach the age of twenty-one, and the apprentice upon admission has to pay the Wardens 6s. 8d., a loaf and two pots of beer. The articles of the company set forth that no one could become a quarryman who was not the son of a quarryman, and for centuries this rule was rigidly kept. Stone used to be shipped at Owre Quay on Poole Harbour, and the right of way to that spot is maintained by kicking a football along the old road after the court is over.

Portland is a royal manor, and still holds its court leet. Among the most important matters dealt with there are the questions of royalties paid by the quarrymen on their stone. All stone exported from the common lands pays a royalty of a shilling a ton, of which one half belongs to the King as lord of the manor, and the other half to the tenants. But in 1665 Charles II made a grant of 3d. a ton from his half to the tenants to reward them for their loyalty in the Civil Wars, and each sovereign since that time has continued this grant.

Dorset Up Along and Down Along (1935)

Naturalists and Naturists at Studland

Studland Bay was ideally suited to support the pirates, mostly outsiders, and the Purbeck families such as Uvedale and Clavell who made or increased their wealth by means of them. Until well into the last century barrels of herrings, kegs of spirits and other goods were stored under piles of seaweed collected for fertiliser, then carried overland to Greenland and Goathorn and loaded into flat-bottomed boats, thus avoiding the well scrutinised Harbour entrance. Little wonder that pirates exploited every possible configuration of intrigue and hypocrisy hereabouts; and always with Studland Bay offering safe anchorage, entertainment, easy victualling by Poole boats, and quick escape in times of emergency, leaving Purbeck men to carry the can and stab one another in the back. Blood certainly was spilt on the boards of the Water Lane hellhouses, and on the silver sands, in the days when cut-throat competition was more than a figure of speech.

The beach seems an altogether more innocent place today. The bloodiest object there is a gory anti-rabies notice whose dripping fangs threaten those who dare to land pets from boats. Beach-huts provide a haven for bathers, and the coastguard's main concern is with the hundreds of small craft that cruise for pleasure. The Bankes Arms, in the village, fills with week-end sailors, though its beer-

garden sports a merchantman's anchor of about 1850, as a reminder
of more serious times. The Manor House Hotel, with its spiky roofs,
turret and round towers, doubtfully commemorates the site of Studland Castle. On the beach below, each tide dispatches bucket-and-
spade castles made from the fine white sand. Waves from the Channel do not maintain sufficient momentum to deposit stones or shingle
on the east-facing coast; but marram grass extends its rhizomes
wherever new sand builds up; as its old leaves are submerged by the
dry, shifting tide, new ones develop at the new surface and the dunes
are continuously consolidated. They are then colonised by sea lyme
and sand-couch grasses, by sea bindweed, saltwort and sheep's bit,
and, beside the nature reserve between the village and Shell Bay, by
sunbathing naturists. Over the last four centuries a series of ridges,
now colonised by heathers and separated by peaty pools, have been
built out of the sea, so that the South Haven peninsula has steadily
grown to its present width. Engulfed in the sandy heath is a stretch of
water, one mile long, called Little Sea, whose western shore was once
coastline.

A map of 1721 shows it as a tidal inlet in a dune ridge; by the
end of the century another ridge had transformed it into a lagoon;
in 1849 the highest spring tides still invaded it, but today it is a
lake rich in freshwater life. Sticklebacks, newts and toads feed cor-
morants and herons; otters are often seen in the waters, and shrews
and harvest mice inhabit the furzy dunes, attracting merlins, spar-
rowhawks, peregrines, hen harriers and other more common birds of
prey to Studland. Warblers breed in the reedbeds where meadow-pipit,
stonechat and linnet can also be seen, while redpolls nest in nearby
silver birches. Sallow graces Little Sea's margins, making a refuge for
the water rail, and yellow flags, bog bean and reed mace are rife at the
water's edge. Some Arthurian souls maintain that it was here that Sir
Bedivere flung Excalibur into the lake's depths, unwittingly crediting
him with remarkable powers of foresight. The only weapons to be
raised above its surface were fowling-pieces from flat-bottomed punts;
and, more recently, powerful binoculars aimed at mallard, pochard,
wigeon, teal and the rest. So sand, Studland's major present-day asset,
has grown into a rich reserve and has shaped the wild and beautiful
beach that attracts twentieth-century hordes.

Paul Hyland (Purbeck, The Ingrained Island, 1978)

Portland

What a wealth of romance has surrounded this West Country promontory since the days of my earliest childhood! Its frowning forehead was familiar to me from Brunswick Terrace in Weymouth, towering above the magpie-speckled lighthouse on the 'old' Breakwater. Rumours of it had reached my ears when I was a very infant. My father used often to appear with round flat pebbles for my mother and grandmother to paint pictures upon, and these, I was told, came from Portland; and when the weather had been particularly wild I would hear of my father and my elder brothers making an excursion to Portland to see the waves!

I cannot conceive of any portion of the English coast more calculated to arouse a boy's imagination than the Chiswell end of the Chesil Beach. It is possible even when the weather is rough to stand in comparative safety and look down into the dragon throat of the terrible bay. A prodigious Atlantic roller, visible for a long time to a rain-drenched onlooker above the turbulence of all lesser waves far out at sea, dashes itself at last against this huge natural breakwater, and a second later, its pride broken, withdraws with an irresistible suction down, down, down, foam and tumbling pebbles together, until with a snarl, the very ocean floor is, for the duration of a moment, exposed under the curved suspended arch of a tottering wall of water, high towering as a church steeple, broad and awe-inspiring as the Niagara in flood.

On a fair summer's morning how wonderful to stand on the famous sea-bank looking out over Dead Man's Bay, with wide-benched deep-water fishing-boats on every side, and the pebbles under foot spotted and blackened with fisherman's tar; the air smelling of green waves, of wind and sunshine; and with vast nets spread out everywhere to dry, loaded with cork floats five times larger in size than those that dangle on the puny spiderweb Weymouth nets, brown nets with a mesh so stout that they could drag to shore an entangled mermaid for all her petulance. And the old stone tavern called the Cove Inn which stands on the top of the beach – was there ever such a hostel? The landlord once told me that during the worst winter gales the sea invariably reaches to its stone porch and goes pouring down on each side of the house to the sheltered village street below. What a view presents it-self from its sarcophagus-like doorway in fine weather – the great sea beach with its widesweeping curve of twenty miles, the broad flecked acres of the West Bay; and everywhere old weather-worn benches, old stone seats, where generations of aged fishermen, with bleared eyes still as keen of sight as the eyes of shags are content to sit for hours scanning a sea and horizon familiar to them for the past seventy or eighty years.

Llewelyn Powys (Dorset Essays, 1935)

A Portland Custom

When I was looking over the quarries in Portland, and attentively considering the operations, observing how soon the quarrymen would cut half a ton of spawls from an unformed block, and what large pieces flew off at every stroke, how speedily their blows followed one another, and how incessantly they pursued this labour, with a tool of from 18 to 20 pounds weight, I was naturally led to view and consider the figure of the operative agent; and after having observed that by far the greatest number of the quarrymen were of a very robust, hardy form, in whose hands the tool I have mentioned seemed a mere plaything, I at last broke out with surprise, and inquired of my guide, Mr. Roper, where they could possibly pick up such a set of stout fellows to handle the kevel, which in their hands seemed nothing; for, I observed, in the space of 15 minutes, they could knock off as much waste matter from a mass of stone, as any of that occupation I had ever seen before would do in an hour. Says Roper, 'We do not go to fetch these from a distance, they are all born upon the island; and many of them have never been further upon the main land than to Weymouth.'

I told him, I thought the air of that island must be very propitious, to furnish a breed of men so particularly formed for the business they followed. 'The air,' he replied, 'though very sharp, from our elevated situation, is certainly very healthy to working men; yet, if you knew how these men are produced, you would wonder the less; for all our marriages here are productive of children.' On desiring an explana-tion how this happened, he proceeded, 'Our people here, as they are bred up to hard labour, are very early in a condition to marry and provide for a family; they intermarry with one another, very rarely going to the main land to seek a wife; and it has been the custom of the island, from time immemorial, that they never marry till the woman is pregnant.'

'But pray,' says I, 'does not this subject you to a great number of bastards? Have not your Portlanders the same kind of fickleness in their attachments that Englishmen are subject to: and in consequence does not this produce many inconveniences?' 'None at all,' replies Roper, 'for previous to my arrival here, there was but one child on record of the parish register that had been born a bastard in the compass of 150 years. The mode of courtship here is, that a young woman never admits of the serious addresses of a young man but on supposition of a thorough probation. When she becomes with child, she tells her mother; the mother tells her father; her father tells his father; and he tells his son, that is then proper time to be married.'

'But suppose, Mr. Roper, she does not prove with child, what happens then; do they live together without marriage, or, if they separate, is not this such an imputation upon her as to prevent her getting another suitor?' 'The case is thus managed,' answered my friend, 'if the woman does not prove with child, after a competent time of courtship, they conclude they are not destined by Providence for each other; they therefore separate; and as it is an established maxim, which the Portland women observe with great strictness, never to admit a plurality of lovers at one time, their honour is no ways tarnished, she just as soon (after the affair is declared to be broke off) gets another suitor as if she had been left a widow, or that nothing had ever happened but that she had remained an immaculate virgin.'

'But pray, Sir, did nothing particular happen upon your men coming down from London?' 'Yes,' says he, 'our men were much struck and mightily pleased with the facility of the Portland ladies; and it was not long before several of the women proved with child; but the men being called upon to marry them, this part of the lesson they were uninstructed in; and, on their refusal, the Portland women arose to stone them out of the island; insomuch that those few who did not choose to take their sweethearts for better or worse, after so fair a trial, were in reality obliged to decamp. On this occasion one bastard only was born; but since then matters have gone on according to the ancient custom.

John Smeaton (*History of the Eddystone Lighthouse, 1791*)

Portland Stone

The good stone is in a stratum below these about twelve feet thick, and there is a sort of flinty stone between the strata. It is in this good vein about the north-west corner they find most petrified shells; the cockle, and oyster, and turben, are most common; they find also many of the heart kind, and some of the Cornu Ammonis. The stones which have the cockle and oyster shell, being close and compact, are fit for foreign use; but those that are full of the turbinated kind and the hearts are not, and they are only used about their own buildings in the island. Under this stratum there is no more good stone; and one sees in the high cliffs that under this it crumbles away and makes heaps of sands on the shoar. The way of drawing it down is by fixing it on a low carriage, to which they chain a large stone, which drags behind on the ground, and they have two horses attended by a man fixed behind the cart, who, when he makes a signal, stand as firm as they can to resist the motion; but when they come to a rapid descent they are dragg'd after the cart, sometimes on their hams. In the north part of the island, to the east of Portland Castle, is a stratum of a black slate from two to six inches thick. This they call a stone coal, for it burns, and they heat their ovens with it; for there is great scarcity of fireing here, insomuch that they make up cowdung mixed with straw, and put it in cakes against the walls of their houses to dry for fewel, as in Egypt; and the same I observ'd along the coast, as far as Abbotsbury.

Richard Pococke (Travels Through England, 1754)

Portland Bill: a Sailor's view

And so for rounding the bill once more – a thing by me always dreaded for Portland Race is a terrible affair.

Portland Race should, by rights, be the most famous thing in all the seas of the world. I will tell you why. It is a dreadful, unexpected, enormous, unique business, set right upon the highway of all our travel: it is the marvel of our seas. And yet it has no fame. There is not a tired man writing with a pencil at top speed in the middle of the night to the shaking of machinery in Fleet Street, who will not use the word 'Maelstrom' or 'Charybdis'. I have seen Charybdis – piffling little thing; I have not seen the Maelstrom, but I have talked to men who told me they had seen it. But Portland Race could eat either of them and not know it had had breakfast.

I have nearly always been successful in catching the smooth, narrow belt near the point: but I also once found that smooth belt fail me, and so have gone through the tail-end of Portland Race; only the very tail-end. I had seen it from close by half a dozen times before in my life. I had very nearly got into it twice. But this time I did actually make knowledge of the 'thing in itself' – and there is no mistaking it. It is one of the wonderful works of God.

Portland Bill stands right out into the Channel and challenges the Atlantic tide. It is a gatepost, with Alderney and the Hogue for gateposts on the other side. They make the gate of the narrow sea; outside them you are really (in spite of names) in the air of the ocean, and look towards the Americas. Inside them is the domestic pond. Portland Bill thrusts out into the Channel and challenges the Atlantic sea. In my folly, for many years I used to call it 'William', but I will do so no longer. For there is something awful about the snake-like descending point, and dreadful menace in the waters beyond. And here Portland Bill differs from his namesake of the land. It would be familiar to call a William of the land 'Bill'. But in the matter of Portland it is familiar to call the Bill 'William'. I will never call him William again.

I thought I had well known what the Race was before I first heard it bellowing years ago. I knew after the fashion of our shadowy nominal knowledge. I knew it in printed letters. I knew it on the chart. I knew it in the *Channel Pilot*. Then I came to it in the flesh, and I knew it by the senses, I saw it with my own eyes, and I had heard it with my ears. I had heard it roaring like a herd, or park, or pride, of lions miles away. I had seen its abominable waste of white water on a calm day: shaving it by a couple of hundred yards. But there is all the difference in the world between that kind of knowledge and knowledge from within!

He that shall go through even the tail-end of Portland Race in a small boat and in calm weather will know what he is talking about, and for so vast an accession of real knowledge, even that pain is worth while. Portland Race lies in a great oval, sometimes three, sometimes four or five miles out from Portland Bill, like a huge pendant hanging from the tip of a demon's ear. It is greater or smaller, according to whether the wind be off-shore or on, but it is immense always, for it is two miles or more across. It lumps, hops, seethes, and bubbles, just like water boiling over the fire, but the jumps are here in feet, and the drops are tons.

There is no set of the sea in Portland Race: no run and sway: no regular assault. It is a chaos of pyramidical waters leaping up suddenly without calculation, or rule of advance. It is not a charge, but a scrimmage; a wrestling bout; but a wrestling bout of a thousand against one. It purposely raises a clamour to shake its adversary's soul, wherein it most resembles a gigantic pack of fighting dogs, for it snarls, howls, yells, and all this most terrifically. Its purpose is to kill, and to kill with a savage pride.

And all these things you find out if you get mixed up in it on a very small boat.

Hilaire Belloc (The Cruise of the Nona, 1925)

This Mother of London

"That," said the quarry foreman, as he included the landscape in a sweep of his hand, "is where St. Paul's came from."

I looked down toward the sea from a high cliff on the eastern side of the Isle of Portland. I saw a valley gouged out of the hill-side: a dead, desolate wilderness; a cutting away of high stone cliffs as if some race of giants had scooped out the stone to its bed, leaving exposed the grey, jagged roots of the rock, now covered here and there with grass and wild flowers.

The foreman turned, pointing downwards towards a cosy bay that lay between steep cliffs with the waves breaking on a shingle beach. "Some of the City churches came out of the great hole! All these old quarries on the east side were worked by Sir Christopher Wren when he rebuilt London. We often find stones quarried in his time and bearing his mark, but rejected for some reason and never shipped to London. Look! This old pillar is said to have been cut for St. Paul's Cathedral; but it never got there!"

I turned to look at a grey pillar, that might have stood on Ludgate Hill, lying covered in brambles that cling closely as if trying to console it for its failure. We walked on together over roads so white with powdered Portland stone that the dust clung like flour to our clothes and formed a grey film on our hands. My guide pointed to a long gash in the rock.

"The Cenotaph!" he remarked casually.

We went on.

"I helped to choose some of the stones for the Cenotaph," he continued. "the top ones with the wreath on them. We picked the purest white stone in the island."

We came at length to a quarry near the sea, in which men were cutting Portland stone. They worked below on stone ledges driving iron bars beneath the stratum; for Portland stone lies in convenient layers. A crane dropped a chain into the quarry. It was attached to the iron wedges, then the crane worked, pulling at the bars till the stone broke into a rough square slab.

On top of the quarry men were shaping these slabs: huge creamy slabs. Portland stone is not white until it has weathered, as you can prove yourself in the Strand any day by comparing new Bush House with ancient Somerset House. Some day Bush House will lose its look of sunburn and grey down to the silver monotone of London.

"Where is all this stone going?" I asked the foreman as we passed between walls of it.

"That," he replied, "is Regent Street!"

Apart from their sentimental interest to all Londoners, the Portland quarries are strange places in which to prowl. You look at a hill-side, and see, plain as in an architect's sectional plan, the strata of which the island is formed. First comes a thin top dressing of soil, below is a deeper stratum of waste stone never used for building which is broken up and thrown into the sea; so that another smaller isle of waste Portland stone four hundred feet high has formed on the west end of the island. Immediately below the waste is a stratum called by the quarrymen the "dirt bed" – a curious grey, knobbly mass like concrete. It is full of fossil fish and trees. I picked out many fine stone mussels, a stone oyster the size of a tea-plate, and the bough of a tree which waved over Portland millions of years ago, so convincing (apart from its weight) that a shortsighted person examining the plainly-marked knots might easily mistake it for wood.

The roots of many of these trees are in the "dirt bed," but the boughs rise up to the stratum of waste stone. Below the dirt bed begins the strata used for building, lying in regular layers.

If you would like to examine the fossils in Portland stone you will see many in the plinth of the King Charles statue at Charing Cross: it is full of sea-shells.

"Will we ever cut the island to the sea level?" repeated my guide, with a laugh. "Not in our time, sir! We reckon that there's enough stone here to last the whole world for another five centuries!"

I thought, in my vanity, that I knew London.

I realize now that no one understands London until he has explored the significant chasms of this white island: this mother of London.

And this I thought: that never again will I look on London with quite the same eyes. Always at the back of my mind will be, as I walk the streets of London, knowledge of a white island lying out to sea like a great whale. When I see Portland stone in London I shall think of the sea breaking against high hills; I shall hear the scream of the gulls, the suck back of pebbles on the little stony beaches; the white dust lying over the road in the little mysterious Isle of London.

H. V. Morton *(In Search of England, 1927)*

The Makeing of Allom

The next Place, that offereth itselfe is Smedmore, where Sir William Clavile, descended of antient Gentrie, built a little newe House, and beatified it with pleasant Gardens. This Place longe sithence had Lordes of the same Name, from whom by *Dolfin* it passed hereditarilie to the *Claviles*, neare adjoineing to the Sea: And not farre hence, the nowe Owner, beeing ingenious in diverse Faculties, put in tryall the Makeing of Allom, which hee had noe sooner, by much Cost and Travell, brought to a reasonable Perfection, but the Farmers of the Allom Workes siezed to the Kings Use; and, beeing not soe skillfull or fortunate as himselfe, were forced with Losses to leave it offe, and soe nowe it rests allmost ruined. But in Place of it *Sir William Clavile*, who one Disaster dismayed not, hath sithence sett up a Glasse House (which is come to Perfection, and is likelie to redounde to a good Benefit) and Salt House.

For Transportation of these Commodities, as alsoe of white Salt (there is made in great Abundance, by boyling it out of the Sea Water) Hee hath at his owne Charge, with great Rocks and Stones piled together, built a little Key in Imitation of that at *Lime*, for small Barkes to ride, invironed on the East Side with an Hill yeelding Myne (as they call it) for the Allom Works, and a kinde of blueish Stones that serve to burne, for maintaineing Fire in the Glass House; but in burneing yeelds such an offensive Savour and extraordinarie Blacknesse, that the People labouring about those Fires are more like Furies than Men.

Coker's Survey of Dorsetshire by Thomas Gerard, (died 1634)

4 · FESTIVE OCCASIONS

Of all the festive occasions celebrated by our ancestors it is Christmas which survives most strongly, though in our largely urban society few children hear the legend of the oxen kneeling at the hour of Christ's birth. Gooding Day (December 21st) seems to have been an offshoot of the Shrove Tuesday tradition when the children of poorer families would call on neighbours for the basic ingredients of a 'feast'.

Royal occasions owed much to the degree of popularity of individual monarchs. Weymouth's devotion to George III extended to his children on their birthdays, and Coronation Day probably inspired its greatest ardour in the prosperous years of Queen Victoria.

The workfolk developed their own festive style in the Whitsun club-walks when the thrift and health clubs paraded, with their banners heading the procession and their bands ready to play the national anthem outside the manor-house or the rectory and country dances on the village green. These club-walks gradually replaced the earlier May Day customs.

Individual towns and villages had and still have their own annual day of festivities associated with the parish's patronal feast-day or a long established fair, such as Sherborne's Pack Monday Fair with its strange accompaniment of 'Teddy Rowe's Band'.

Christmas Customs

The Rev. A.H. Baverstock, for many years Rector of Hinton Martel, writes of an old custom formerly kept up in that parish on the feast of St. Thomas (December 21st). This day was known as Gooding Day, and the children sang a song about coming a gooding and begging for ingredients for the Christmas pudding. He says: 'I always used to give them a penny after Church on that day to keep the idea alive.'

At Christmas time the old mumming play of St. George and the Turkish Knight was acted in many parts of Dorset, but the custom broke down during the war years, 1914-18, although it has occasionally been revived at Evershot since that period.

Mummers at Shillingstone survived only until the late seventies of the last century, but the men and boys of the village kept up the ancient and terrifying custom of the Bull until a rather later date.

The Bull, shaggy head with horns complete, shaggy coat, and eyes of glass, was wont to arrive, uninvited at any Christmas festivity. None knew when he might or might not appear. He was given the freedom of every house, and allowed to penetrate into any room escorted by his keeper. The whole company would flee before his formidable horns, the more so as, towards the end of the evening, neither the bull nor his keeper could be certified as strictly sober. The Christmas Bull is now obsolete, but up to forty years ago, he was a recognized custom. In some parts of West Dorset this creature was known as the Wooser, and there are those who tell us that he has his origin in Devil-worship.

Dorset Up Along and Down Along, 1935

The Oxen

Christmas Eve, and twelve of the clock.
  'Now they are all on their knees,'
An elder said as we sat in a flock
  By the embers in hearthside ease.

We pictured the meek mild creatures where
    They dwelt in their strawy pen,
Nor did it occur to one of us there
    To doubt they were kneeling then.

So fair a fancy few would weave
    In these years! Yet, I feel,
If someone said on Christmas Eve,
    'Come; see the oxen kneel

'In the lonely barton by yonder coomb
    Our childhood used to know,'
I should go with him in the gloom,
    Hoping it might be so.

Thomas Hardy (1915)

A Royal Birthday

This being the anniversary of the birth of her Royal Highness, the Duchess of Wurtemburg, their Majesties' eldest daughter, the morning was ushered in with the usual demonstrations of joy.

The King, Queen, and all the Princesses, with a number of the Nobility went to Maiden Castle near Dorchester, to see the sports of the country people. The sports were announced in the following handbill:

"All persons of jovial, friendly, and loyal disposition are invited to be present at, and to partake of the under-mentioned country sports, which with others to be declared upon the ground are intended, if the weather is fine, to be exhibited at Maiden Castle, near Dorchester, this day at eleven o'clock in the morning, in honour of her Royal Highness, the Duchess of Wurtemburg.

"To be played for at cricket, a round of beef: each man of the winning set to have a ribband.

"A Cheese to be rolled down the hill, prize to whoever stops it.

"A Silver Cup to be run for by Ponies, the best of three heats.

"A pound of tobacco to be grinned for.

"A barrel of beer to be rolled down the hill; prize to whoever stops it.

"A Michaelmas goose to be dived for.

"A good hat to be cudgelled for.

"Half a guinea for the best ass in three heats.

"A handsome hat for the boy most expert in catching a roll dipped in treacle and suspended by a string.

"A leg of mutton and a gallon of porter to the winner of a race of one hundred yards in sacks.

"A good hat to be wrestled for.

"Half a guinea to the rider of the ass who wins the best of three heats by *coming* in last.

"A pig, prize to whoever catches him by the Tail."

The Times, *Sept. 30, 1798.*

Royal Fêtes

That year [1798] there was a rural fête given on Maiden Castle, a British Camp, close to Monkton where my uncle resided. I went to stay a few days at his house at this time. We walked, a party of us, to the ground. Every regiment had a marquee pitched, with refreshments. The sports were: grinning through a horse-collar, jumping in sacks, catching a pig by the tail, which said tail had been previously shaved and greased, donkey racing, the last donkey to be the winner; rolls dipped in treacle suspended by strings to be devoured by boys with their hands tied behind them; diving for apples in a meal-tub; Le mat de Coc; women racing for under garments, with other rural sports made Royal for the occasion. Speaking of Royal Fêtes, I will mention another in order to give the vulgar an idea how royally things were done in this way. The Queen ordained a Fête, and the Princess Elizabeth planned it, and the Princess Amelia wrote verses for the occasion. Lord Sudley, the Acting Manager, was sent to all the tradespeople who dealt in ornamental wares, ordering them, in the Queen's name, to erect Booths in a certain field near the Radipole Barracks, and therein to display their goods as at a Village Fair. Several of the Actors were engaged to play various parts; among the rest Penly, dressed as a cook and mounted on an ass, met the Royal Family on their entrance and sung out a bill of fare written by the Princess Amelia. Then there were Lotteries and Whirligigs, where it was contrived that His Most Gracious Majesty should win a penny raffle for his prize.

Well, it all went off, doubtless, very satisfactorily; and a few days after Lord Sudley was again sent round to *reward* the tradespeople for their trouble. Mr. Harvey who was a watch maker and jeweller, as well as being the proprietor of the large Library on the Esplanade, had sent trinkets to the value of many hundreds, and his wife was paid for the risk and trouble by the munificent sum of *half a guinea*. This I heard from her own lips. She dared not refuse it, for it would not do to affront Royalty. At this last Fête my father had the *honour* of being introduced to the Queen, I ought to say *presented* by the King himself. And whilst enumerating Royal *Honours*, I must not forget to mention that the King, who always spoke very loud, was once heard to say on the Esplanade that Mrs. Ham was 'decidedly the finest woman in Weymouth'.

Elizabeth Ham (1798)

Coronation Day

June 28. Being Coronation Day there are games and dancing on the green at Sturminster Newton. The stewards with white rosettes. One is very anxious, fearing that while he is attending to the runners the leg-of-mutton on the pole will go wrong; hence he walks hither and thither with a compressed countenance and eyes far ahead.

The pretty girls, just before a dance, stand in inviting positions on the grass. As the couples in each figure pass near where their immediate friends loiter, each girl-partner gives a laughing glance at such friends, and whirls on.

Thomas Hardy (1877)

May Day and Club-Walking

At Sherborne, on May Day in former times the children would come round with garlands; they decorated themselves with chains of flowers and wore wreaths and chanted a song, which began with the words:–
'The first of May
Is garland day
Please to remember
The King and Queen.'
At Shaftesbury they used to carry about 'Jack in the Greens' and ask

for pennies. At Wyke Regis and Abbotsbury on May 13th and 14th the children used to make garlands of flowers and skip with them through the street and then hang them on the fishing boats. When the boats went to sea, the garlands were thrown overboard into the waters of West Bay.

During the nineteenth century the village feast or club-walking had largely taken the place of the old May Day festivities. With the growth of national friendly societies, old age pensions and health insurance, the old village clubs have now died out for the most part.

Ninety years ago the Lytchett Matravers Club was a flourishing one. Their feast day was Trinity Monday when all the members turned out in their best clean smocks and gay neckerchiefs and carrying and wearing garlands. There was a prize for the best garland of flowers. They first marched to church and had a service; then they formed a procession carrying garlands and their club signs (in this village the emblems were of painted wood, not brass) and went round to collect from the farmers. A band led them which must have existed chiefly for this purpose, as there always used to be one, and it has died out since the club ceased. Having given the farmers a tune, they marched to the inn at Higher Lytchett where there was a great and solid meal awaiting them. This was well washed down with cider and beer, and then maypole and country dancing was kept up till late at night, and crowds of folk came from all round in coaches and waggons to watch. Stalls were put up too, 'almost like a fair,' they said.

Dorset Up Along and Down Along, 1935

Fairs and Parish Festivities

St. Michael's Fair or Pack Monday Fair, which is held on the second Monday of October at Sherborne, was predominantly a sheep fair. A hundred years ago it was already decreasing in size. In 1828 the *Dorset County Chronicle* reported: "Sherborne Fair, on Monday last, was fully attended, the weather being particularly fine. The supply of sheep was unusually small, the number of sheep and lambs penned amounting only to about 9,000, which were nearly all sold."

This fair is heralded by a queer old custom. In the very early hours a band of townspeople parade the streets of Sherborne beating upon tea-trays, frying-pans, bugles and whistles. This is 'Teddy Rowe's

Band.' The figures striding by in the moonlight accompanied by the unearthly din have a very strange effect. The origin of the custom is not known, but it is said to have begun upon the completion of certain restoration work at the Abbey in the fifteenth century. Horns used to be sold in the shops at this time so that the band should be well supplied, and boys would buy cow-horns from the butchers and fashion home-made instruments upon which to blow.

Woodbury Hill Fair, the largest in Dorset, was held on the hill just outside Bere Regis. Traders came from distant parts, and the fair used to last for five days. The first was 'Wholesale' day, and the second 'Gentlefolks' day, when oysters were eaten. The third was 'Allfolks' Day, the fourth 'Sheepfair' Day and Friday was 'Pack and Penny' Day when all the goods remaining were offered at a great reduction.

Fairs which were held at rather remote places, on the patronal festival of the parish church, or on some other holy day, probably always had more of the character of a holiday, and less of a serious economic nature than others.

Dorset Up Along and Down Along, 1935

Firmity Sunday and Harvest Home

A resident of Whitechurch Canonicorum remembers the making of firmity. 'It was generally made after the harvest, of wheat, raisins, currants and a little flour to thicken it. These were slowly boiled and sweetened with a little sugar, and it was then eaten like porridge with a spoon. It was usually made on a Sunday called Firmity Sunday.'

The harvest home supper was a great time for songs and dancing. A typical drinking song is recorded at Marnhull:–

'Here's a health unto our Master, the founder of the feast.
I hope to God wi' all me heart his soul in Heaven may rest.
And all his works may prosper, whatever he takes in hand
For we are all his servants, and here at his command.
Then drink boys drink, and see you do not spill,
For if you do, you shall drink two, it is our Master's will.
Here's a health unto our Master, our Mistress shan't go free;
For she's a good provider, provides as well as he;
For she's a good provider, and bids us all to come,

So take this cup and sip it up, for 'tis our harvest home,
Fill it up to the brim, and drink it off clane,
For 'tis our harvest home.'

Dorset Up Along and Down Along, 1935

Dorset Cider

No, no, I don't hold wi' these coloured waters,
Martinis, cocktails, and other such.
Maybe they're fit for the gentry's daughters;
They're not for you and me to touch.
No, if 'tis to do 'ee good,
Cider's the stuff, drawn cool from the wood.

Oh, a drap of ale's all right, I tell 'ee,
Puts back the sweat that's lost on a farm;
And beer feeds blood and fills the belly –
Never did nobody any harm....
But there, 'tis not a drink, 'tis *food*!
Cider's the stuff, drawn cool from the wood.

Spirits? Well, brandy's a great reliever
If you're feelin' faint, or sour wi' yourself;
And Whisky-an'-lemon can staunch a fever -
I keep a drench of it on my shelf.
But where drinkin' is really understood,
Cider's the stuff, drawn cool from the wood.

And different again as church from chapel,
These fancy Wines from oversea.
French grape or English apple?
No two minds where my choice would be....
Ay, nothin' beats it, nor never could –
Darset cider, drawn cool from the wood!

Clive Sansom ('Landlord – The Black Bear' in Dorset Village, 1962)

5 · HARD TIMES

Like most other places Dorset has known dark days in its history when life itself was threatened by some widespread disaster or invasion by an enemy or the unremitting privations of poverty. In the fourteenth century it was the Black Death which reached Weymouth, or Melcombe as it was then known, from the mainland of Europe and decimated the county as it spread into England.

Weymouth was again overwhelmed with fear of unimaginable perils in the opening years of the nineteenth century when Napoleon's 'army of England' was poised at Boulogne to force a landing on the Dorset coast and invade the country. Badbury Rings was one of the beacons prepared to be set on fire as a signal if the French came ashore. The false alarm of 1804 created a panic that Elizabeth Ham vividly described in her autobiography. Later in the nineteenth century it was the less spectacular but no less terrible impact of poverty and starvation, riot and oppression, that strained to breaking point the mutual interdependence of landowner, tenant and farmworkers – culminating in the shabby trial and transportation of the Tolpuddle Martyrs.

Even in a calmer atmosphere the daily life of the humble cottager was distinctly austere, with one's daily bread dependent on success in gleaning the fallen grain in the empty fields after harvest.

The Plague Reaches England

The plague first attacked England in the autumn of 1348.

Rumours of the coming scourge reached England in the early summer. On August 17th, 1348, the Bishop of Bath and Wells, Ralph of Shrewsbury, sent letters through his diocese ordering "processions and stations every Friday, in each collegiate, regular, and parish church, to beg God to protect the people from the pestilence which had come from the East into the neighbouring kingdom." and granting an indulgence of forty days to all who, being in a state of grace, should give alms, fast or pray, in order, if possible, to avert God's anger.

The "neighbouring kingdom" spoken of by the Bishop in his letter may be taken almost certainly to refer to France. From Calais it is probable that the pestilence was brought into England in certain ships conveying some who were anxious to escape from it. Most of the contemporary accounts agree in naming the coast of Dorsetshire as the part first infected. Thus Galfrid le Baker, a contemporary, says "it came first to a seaport in Dorsetshire, and then into the country, which it almost deprived of inhabitants, and from thence it passed into Devon and Somerset to Bristol." Two or three of the chronicles, also, more particular than the rest, name Melcombe Regis as the memorable spot where the epidemic first showed itself in England. "In the year of our Lord 1348, about the feast of the Translation of St. Thomas (July 7th)," writes the author of the chronicle known as the *Eulogium Historiarum*, who was a monk of Malmesbury at this time, "the cruel pestilence, terrible to all future ages, came from parts over the sea to the south coast of England, into a port called Melcombe, in Dorsetshire. This [plague] sweeping over the southern districts, destroyed numberless people in Dorset, Devon, and Somerset." So, too, a continuation of Trivet's chronicle, taken down to the death of Edward III, by a canon of Bridlington, who was thus probably a contemporary of the event, says that "the great plague came into England to the southern districts, beginning by some [ships] putting in from the sea into a town called Melcombe."

Melcombe Regis, or Weymouth, was at that time a port of considerable importance. No evidence is known to exist as to the mortality in the port itself; but an item of information as to the effect of the disease in the neighbourhood is afforded at a subsequent period. Three years after the plague had passed, the King, by his letters patent, forbade any of the inhabitants of the island of Portland to leave their homes there, or, indeed, to sell any of their crops out of the district, "because," he says, "as we have learnt, the island of Portland, in the county of Dorset, has been so depopulated in the time of the late pestilence that the inhabitants remaining are not sufficiently numerous to protect it against our foreign enemies. . . ."

Francis Aidan Gasquet (The Great Pestilence), 1893

Badbury Rings: The Beacon

Milton Abbey, Blandford
Oct 12th 1803

My dear Bankes.

The spring tides take place next Saturday, and the information to Government is so precise that the Isle of Wight is the enemy's object that it is not improbable they may avail themselves of this ensuing spring-tide; if they do not, their attempt must be postponed another month. Under these circumstances I would not fail of giving you this notice, in confidence that you will keep it to yourself, & only so far prepare Mrs Banks & your family as to be able to remove them upon the first intelligence of the enemy's being off the coast. I have to beg of you that you will give directions for an assemblage of fagots, furze & other fuel, also straw to be stacked & piled on the summit of Badbury Rings, so as the whole may take fire instantly & the fire be maintained for two hours. The general direction if you will take the trouble of ordering the execution is that this beacon may be fired whenever the beacon off St Catherine's (Christ Church) is fired to the eastward, or whenever the beacons on Lytchett Heath or Woodbury Hill, are fired to the westward, but not from the demonstration of any coast signal.

I am, my dear Bankes,
Yours most sincerely
Dorchester.

A letter from Earl of Dorchester (*1803*) in *The Story of Corfe Castle, George Bankes*

Invasion

The season of 1804 has left but a dull picture of my memory. The most stirring event was an alarm of Invasion. (Napoleon had collected 150,000 men, 'the army of England', at Boulogne.)

Old Mr Mansell and my brother John happened to be with us, when one morning very early the latter came and tapped at my father's door, which was close to mine, to tell him the French Fleet was off the coast. This I heard, and immediately began to dress. Mr Mansell was disturbed by the noise and opening his door called out, 'What's the matter, John?' 'The French are landing in the West Bay,' he replied. 'Oh, d-m 'em; let's be at 'em,' said the old man hurrying on his clothes.

In a few minutes Drums were beating to arms. Officers galloping about in all directions. The horses being put to the Royal Carriages, and everybody standing at their doors asking everybody for news. I was soon dressed and down, and the first person I encountered was the servant girl with the sweeping brush in her hand hurrying to the front door. 'Where are you going, Sally?' said I. 'Oh, Miss Bessy, I am going away, I won't stop a minute longer!' 'Well put down the brush first,' said I, 'you need not take that with you at all events.' Seeing me take it so coolly, she paused a little to consider. The next minute Mary appeared, then a slip of a girl about twelve, with her bonnet and cloak on and her gloves in her hand. 'How are we to go, Bessy? Why don't you get ready?' The next minute Frederick Mansell who with his wife was staying with a family near, came across to ask for a place for his wife, supposing we should harness old Jewel to the Cart, well knowing that no conveyance could be hired.

Nothing more was known all this time but that under cover of a dense fog, the French were landing somewhere. That there was real cause for alarm no one could doubt, who witnessed the anxious looks of the hurrying Field Officers, and saw the Royal Carriages drawn up in front of Gloster Lodge, ready to start at a moment's notice. Still the fog hung its dense veil over the threatened mischief, and mystery and suspense added ten-fold force to the alarm. All that could be learnt was this. Soon after dawn some Portland fishermen had landed on that Island with the report that having been out looking after their nets they were lost in the fog. When all at once they found themselves in the midst of a large Fleet of armed ships. They pulled with all their might, and it was fortunately towards land. A certain Mr. Daniel who had recently purchased some stone-quarries in the Island, was awakened, and taking horse galloped to the Ferry and brought the news to Weymouth, declaring that the shots were making the pebbles fly about him as he rode along Chessel bank. Of course there were Sentinels stationed along the shore but as there was no attempt to land on that part up to nine or ten o'clock it was concluded that the Enemy was trying some other part of the Coast.

By this time troops of Yeomanry were galloping into the Town. Everybody still at their doors asking everybody for further news. About twelve o'clock the fog thought proper to lift up its awful curtain and to disclose to all eager eyes strained seaward, first the frigates and Royal Yachts with sails all set and ready for action, then a clear expanse of smooth unruffled water without another speck of canvas in sight. The French Fleet had vanished, 'and like the baseless fabric of a vision left not a wreck behind'. Poor Mr. Daniel hid himself behind his Portland Stone for weeks after.

Elizabeth Ham (1798)

Bannocks and Gleaning

Memories of hard times linger still among the descendants of those who were the chief sufferers. In 1930 one of the older members of the Ashmore Institute said : 'In my parents' young days bread was very dear, so they used to eat barley cake (bannock as it was called). My grandmother would buy barley meal which was cheaper than barley flour. She would put it through a range (or as we say, a sieve) to get the flour out to make the cakes and they would eat them with treacle or blue cheese. The latter could be bought for 4d. a lb.'

The bannock or barley cake was baked in a round crock hung over the fire. Tea was 5/- a lb. They used to make it go further with a baked crust crumbled up in it.

It was only possible to have wheaten bread after the women had been leasing (or gleaning). This custom largely died out with the introduction of mechanical harvesters which leave few ears of corn behind them. A Winterbourne Kingston contributor wrote in 1930 : 'When I was a young woman and lived at Kingston, I used to come over to

Anderson for leasing as there was more to be got there. No one might go leasing unless she had a father or brother working on the farm. We used to send the wheat to the mill to be ground. We did not pay money for the grinding, but the miller used to take toll, sometimes in bread, sometimes in so many lbs. of flour. Some families got enough by leasing to make all their bread for the year. I knew one woman who got three sacks herself. We used to make the bread at home, and bake it in a brick oven. The oven had wood put into it, not too much at a time, till it was hot enough. Then the wood was raked out and the bread put in. Gorse is the best wood for heating the oven.'

Dorset Up Along and Down Along, 1935

The Farm Labourers' Revolt, 1830

As the month of November advanced it became very gloomy, more than its proverbial horrors ever displayed before. An universal spirit of dissatisfaction pervaded every class. The plentiful harvest, good potato crop, remarkably fine autumn weather without frost to impede the labours of husbandry, appeared to have no effect in lessening the murmurs of discontent; whilst incendiaries, whose steps could not be traced, spread rapidly from Kent – where the setting fire to corn-stacks, barns, etc., first began in the month of October – to the adjacent counties. These incendiarisms were in general unconnected with the riotous mobs which nearly at the same time assembled, breaking and destroying machinery used in husbandry, paper-mills, etc., and also surrounding gentlemen's houses, extorting money and demanding an increase of wages. These mobs rose very unexpectedly, and spread with alarming rapidity.

On the 22nd of November the first risings took place in this county. Mr Portman immediately promised to raise the wages of his labourers, and by doing this without concert with other gentlemen, greatly increased their difficulties. My brother, Frampton, harangued the people at Bere Regis, and argued with them on the impropriety of their conduct, refusing to concede to their demands whilst asked with menaces. This spirited conduct caused him to be very unpopular, and threats were issued against him and his house.

November 28th. – Notice was received of an intended rising of the people at the adjacent villages of Winfrith, Wool, and Lulworth – the latter six miles off – which took place on the 30th. My brother, Mr. Frampton, was joined very early on that morning by a large body of farmers, etc., from his immediate neighbourhood, as well as some from a distance, all special constables, amounting to upwards of 150, armed only with a short staff, the pattern for which had been sent by order of Government to equip what was called the Constabulary force. The numbers increased as they rode on towards Winfrith, where the clergyman was unpopular, and his premises supposed to be in danger. The mob, urged on from behind hedges, etc., by a number of women and children, advanced rather respectfully, and with their hats in their hands, to demand increase of wages, but would not listen to the request that they would disperse. The Riot Act was read. They still urged forwards, and came close up to Mr. Frampton's horse; he then collared one man, but in giving him in charge he slipped from his captors by leaving his smock-frock in their hands. Another mob from Lulworth were said to be advancing, and as the first mob seemed to have dispersed, Mr. F. was going, almost alone, to speak to them, when he was cautioned to beware, as the others had retreated only to advance again with more effect in the rear. The whole body of the constabulary then advanced with Mr. Frampton, and, after an ineffectual parley, charged them, when three men were taken, and were conveyed by my brother and his son Henry, and a part of the constabulary force, to Dorchester, and committed to gaol. I was at Moreton that day. Our gentlemen returned about six o'clock; they described the mob they had encountered as being in general very fine-looking young men, and particularly well-dressed, as if they had put on their best clothes for the occasion. Many threats had been reported to us as having been made in the course of the day, and, during the dispersion of the mob, against Mr. Frampton's person and property, but no fire took place on his estate. There was one announced to us watchers, but not being very near to Moreton, we had nothing to do but to lament over the wickedness which occasioned that and so many other incendiary fires.

There were no soldiers in the county, all having been sent towards London, Wiltshire, and Hampshire, where the riots raged first; and in the beginning of December hourly accounts of the assembling of mobs, for the purpose of breaking thrashing-machines, increase of wages, and extorting money, etc., arrived. Under these circumstances, it was judged necessary to block up all the lower windows of Moreton

House, as well as all the doors, with the exception of that to the offices. The Mayor of Dorchester ordered the staff of Dorset Militia to go to Moreton to defend the house, nightly patrols were established, and Mr. Frampton or his son sat up alternately for many nights.

The town of Dorchester was well patrolled. No rising took place there or at Fordington; on the contrary, the latter were most active in extinguishing a fire at a place a mile distant where, however, two ricks of corn were burnt. A troop of lancers arrived at Dorchester about this time, December 12th, and were joyfully received. Most of the thrashing machines in this neighbourhood were, however, either laid aside or destroyed by the farmers themselves, and no rising occurred very near Dorchester. The troop of lancers looked worn down by the fatigues of the riots in Wiltshire, but were immediately called upon to guard old Mrs. William's house at Castle Hill, upon which an attack had been threatened. This troop was soon relieved by three troops of 3rd Dragoon Guards, who were placed permanently in the barracks at Dorchester. About seventy prisoners were at different times committed to gaol, and mobs and tumults became rare occurrences. But, alas! the fires still continued at intervals, and no clue in this county any more than in others could be found by which to detect the perpetrators.

Our Christmas was passed with a large family party at Moreton. The house was unbarred and unblockaded with the exception of the one large window on the staircase. The carol singers from Mr. Frampton's own parishes ushered in Christmas Eve and Christmas Morn as usual, but no mummers were allowed to perform their ancient drama of the wonderful recovery of a man killed in battle by a little bottle of elixir drawn from the pocket of the doctor of the piece, or to personify the "Senses" from the ancient mysteries with their Latin names, "Tactus," "Visus," etc. The yule log, however, burnt on the large hearth of the entrance hall. The peacock in full plumage with its fiery mouth was placed on the dinner table, with of course the boar's head; the immense candles were well covered with laurel. The hare appeared with the red herring astride on its back, and the wassail bowl and lamb's wool were not inferior to former years.

The Journal of Mary Frampton, 1885

The Tolpiddle Martyrs

Ralph Wightman, who was reared and eventually buried in the valley of the river Piddle and spent much of his life as a resident of Piddletown, insisted on using the old name, Piddle; as did John Byng, Viscount Torrington, in his 1782 diary reference to his visit to 'Piddleton'. The Victorians reputedly sanitised the name to spare the blushes of the young ladies who dealt with telegrams in Puddletown post-office.

From Dorchester the main London road continues along the Piddle valley, past the lovely old manor-house at Athelhampton and through the watermeadows for two miles to Tolpiddle. The heath is always away on the right and the cultivated land on the left.

Tolpiddle is like Piddletown in giving its name to one of the heaths, while getting its living from the valley and the chalk hills. There is a grand church, wonderfully sited by the side of the quiet waters, but Tolpiddle's chief claim to fame is that it was the home of the Tolpiddle Martyrs and the birthplace of the Trade Union Movement. In 1833-34 George Loveless and five other agricultural workers banded themselves together to ask for a living wage. There was nothing very revolutionary about their object, and there is no doubt that they were all honest, hardworking men. Loveless was a local preacher associated with the Tolpiddle Nonconformist chapel, but this evidence of unorthodox Christian belief was probably an additional fault in the view of the squires and farmers of his day. It is within my own memory that being a "chapel man" implied that you were also "a ranting Radical". At any rate Loveless and his companions were arrested and tried for conspiracy at Dorchester. Accounts of the trial indicate that the court was grossly prejudiced against them, and they were sentenced to transportation for seven years. Then followed something which restores one's faith in the essential decency of the English. There was such a popular outcry that they were allowed to return to England in 1838. It should be noted that there was no organised Left Wing party in those days. The men who spoke in Parliament to obtain the pardon of the Martyrs were of the same class and of the same education as their unjust judges.

On the 27th of May, 1912, a memorial arch was erected at the entrance to the tiny bare chapel in Tolpiddle where most of the men had worshipped. This arch was built by the Wesleyans and the Trade Unions.

Ralph Wightman (The Wessex Heathland, 1953)

The Statement of George Loveless

As to the trial, I need not mention but little; the cowardice and dastardly conduct throughout are better known by all that were present than could be by any description that I can give of it: suffice it to say, the most unfair and unjust means were resorted to in order to frame an indictment against us; the grand jury appeared to ransack heaven and earth to get some clue against us, but in vain; our characters were investigated from our infancy to the then present moment; our masters were inquired of to know if we were not idle, or attended public houses, or some other faults in us; and much as they were opposed to us, they had common honesty enough to declare that we were good labouring servants, and that they never heard of any complaint against us; and when nothing whatever could be raked together, the unjust and cruel judge, Williams, ordered us to be tried for mutiny and conspiracy, under an act 37 Geo. III., cap. 123, for the suppression of mutiny amongst the marines and seamen, a number of years ago, at the Nore.

The greater part of the evidence against us, on our trial, was put into the mouths of the witnesses by the judge; and when he evidently wished them to say any particular thing, and the witness would say, "I cannot remember," he would say, "Now think; I will give you another minute to consider;" and he would then repeat over the words, and ask, "Cannot you remember?" Sometimes, by charging them to be careful what they said, by way of intimidation, they would merely answer, "yes;" the judge would set it down as the witness's words.

I shall not soon forget the address of the judge to the jury, in summing up the evidence: among other things, he told them, that if such Societies were allowed to exist, it would ruin masters, cause a stagnation in trade, destroy property, and if they should not find us guilty, he was certain they would forfeit the opinion of the grand jury. I thought to myself, there is no danger but we shall be found guilty, as we have a special jury for the purpose, selected from among those who are most unfriendly towards us – the grand jury, landowners, the petty jury, land-renters. Under such a charge, from such a quarter, self-interest alone would induce them to say, "Guilty."

The judge then inquired if we had anything to say. I instantly forwarded the following short defence, in writing, to him:- "My Lord, if we have violated any law, it was not done intentionally: we have injured no man's reputation, character, person, or property: we were uniting together to preserve ourselves, our wives, and our children, from utter degradation and starvation. We challenge any man, or number of men, to prove that we have acted, or intend to act, different from the above statement." The judge asked if I wished it to be read in Court. I answered, "Yes." It was then mumbled over to a part of the jury, in such an inaudible manner, that although I knew what was there, I could not comprehend it. And here one of the counsel prevented sentence being passed, by declaring that not one charge brought against any of the prisoners at the bar was proved, and that if we were found guilty a great number of persons would be dissatisfied; "and I shall for one," said he.

Two days after this we were again placed at the bar to receive sentence, when the judge told us, "that not for any thing that we had done, or, as he could prove, we intended to do, but for an example to others, he considered it his duty to pass the sentence of seven years' transportation across his Majesty's high seas upon each and every one of us."

We arrived at Portsmouth about nine o'clock at night, and I was given up in charge to the officers of the York Hulk. When I went on board I was struck with astonishment at the sight of the place, the clinking of the chains, and of so many men being stripped. When ordered to put on the hulk livery, and called upon to attend on the smith to have the fetters rivetted on my legs, for a moment I began to sink down, until the first mate, a Mr. Nicholson, told me I was to go into No. 9 ward, middle deck, one of the best and quietest wards in the ship, and that I was to go there by the captain's order, in consequence of a good character he had received with me from the prison.

And yet, after all the striving and struggling by my adversaries, to discover some foul blot against my reputation, without effect, so cruel and reckless for revenge was some party, as to say that I and my brother were rioters; now, to prove the fallacy of such an assertion, I would just refer to the period already alluded to, when we asked our employers to advance our wages, no threats or intimidations were made use of by any of the labourers; and, at the time when so much incendiarism was prevailing in many parts of the kingdom, a watch was set in our parish for the protection of property in the night, and I and my brother, among others, was chosen to watch such property. Will any reasonable man believe, if we had been rioters, that we should have been so chosen!

Again, I and my brother were reported to have been regular smugglers and poachers. But all this reporting, stabbing, and slandering men was in the dark, behind the back, out of sight; and well did the party know that there was no foundation for such foul and black assertions, and if there ever was an instance known in the space of thirty-seven years, which was my age when these vile slanders went abroad; I say, if ever, in any one instance, I stand chargeable for any misdemeanour or crime, I call upon James Frampton, Esq., or his satellites, or any one else, to stand out and declare it.

Again, I challenge them to come forth and do it in a public manner, that the world may judge the case, and acquit me if innocent, or not let me escape with impunity if guilty. But the secret is this; I am from principle, a Dissenter, and by some, in Tolpuddle, it is considered as the sin of witchcraft; nay, there is no forgiveness for it in this world nor that which is to come; the years 1824-5 are not forgotten, and many a curious tale might be told of men that were persecuted, banished, and not allowed to have employ if they entered the Wesleyan Chapel at Tolpuddle. But enough of this subject, it is still on record.

George Loveless, (Victims of Whiggery, London 1837)

Cottages near Creech.

6 · THE HEATH

There are many individually named heaths extending eastwards from Dorchester to the New Forest and beyond, but within Dorset they tend now to be known by the collective name given to them by Thomas Hardy in The Return of the Native *– Egdon Heath. He was born and reared on the edge of heathland, at Higher Bockhampton, and the landscape of the uncultivated 'waste' had for him the same depth of meaning and emotion that the Lake District had for Wordsworth. It was the wilderness refuge of the scapegoat, the outcast, the prophet.*

To the agricultural improvers of the eighteenth century the heath's unprofitable character was almost a challenge to their virility. Over the past two hundred years about 85% of the Dorset heathland has been civilised, yielding its incorrigible acres to plantations of conifers, housing estates, military tank-training grounds and an atomic energy establishment among other enterprises, at the expense of its poetic character and its rare and remarkable ecology.

Egdon Heath: Three Views

Near Piddletown begins a large tract of heathy ground, which from thence eastwards occupies a great part of the southern coast, and extends to Hampshire and Surrey, and to the great heaths beyond London. This is professedly the most barren part of the county; and Nature, who has in other parts distributed her beauties with so liberal a hand, seems here, by way of contrast, to exhibit a view of all others the most dreary and unpleasing.

John Hutchins (1774)

This strange and unique fragment of Britain's landscape is as irreplaceable as a Gothic cathedral.

Christopher Booker: a letter to The Times *newspaper (1982)*

Civilisation was its enemy.

Thomas Hardy (The Return of the Native, *1878)*

Hardy's Cottage and the Heath

I went to Higher Bockhampton on an April morning when all the good chalk land of Stinsford was happy with hope. In the arable fields the green of the young crops of oats and barley was a blessing to the eye; the cattle were grazing the first growth of spring in deep pastures, and the cherry trees were in blossom. The lowest boughs in the brushwood sheaf round the elm-tree bole were in tiny leaf. Everywhere on the good land there was a miracle of the resurrection. Behind Hardy's house the heath was still barren. Last year's dead bracken hid any sign of green. The heather was almost black. Only the lovely useless silver birch was in bud and there was golden blossom on the thick spikes of the gorse.

The front of the old house was a garden of lawns and flower-beds and blossoming shrubs. The crowding trees round it had felt the touch of spring, but the heath behind the blank back wall was lifeless and forbidding. I had never realised before that the back wall was without the windows of a living-room. If Hardy had gone out in the evening he would have had no friendly light across the waste to guide him home. All the lights were shining towards the fertile valley.

I walked in the heath along the back of the house and followed the line of the trees between the good land and the wilderness. They were poor trees, over-ripe and valueless for timber. The sun shone on roots covered in thick moss. The track was thick with the leafmould of centuries. Some trunks were dead on the ground, others leaning perilously with half their roots exposed, others had snapped halfway from the top. A thicket of suckers had started to take the place of the forest, and although it was lovely it was very desolate. It may be that I was glad that a few such bits of primeval woodland should remain in our domesticated England, but I realised that a forestry expert might see it only as a tragedy, just as I would see good farmland covered by the purple beauty of thistles.

The fringe of the old woodland is narrow at this point on the heath. East-ward there is a tumbled waste, broken by modern plantations of dark conifers. It is a feature of all this part of Egdon that you can hardly walk twenty yards without coming on one of those strange pits – perfect inverted cones, often forty feet deep – which differ fundamentally from any pit made by man. All over the heathland there are pits from which gravel has been dug. Most of them have ragged boundaries, whereas the natural pits are beautifully regular, but the one point about a man-made pit is that it has an entrance. The gravel pits on the heath have a way in which is wide enough to take a cart. The chalk pits on the downs have a narrow twisting track for a donkey carrying panniers. The natural pits of the heath have no entrance at all. Many of them are old enough to have grown trees; in fact in some the trees have grown, and fallen, and died in the bottom. If young Hardy wandered into one of these pits – and he could not have avoided it within a hundred yards of his home – he would have seen the kindly earth shut out and nothing remaining but the twilight of his pagan gods.

The heath does not retard the dawn and shut out the spring. It is a very small place in reality, but it is very old and it has never been marked with water and the sign of the cross. The old gods live here, the Immortals, the pagan Fates which made such play with Tess, the whole torturing range of human frailties, the tortuous dim horrors which for Hardy obscured the decent ordinary world. Every inch of the heath is twisted and riven into senseless shapes. There are these pits which hold no water and valleys which grow no green pastures. There are hills which give no prospect and brooks which end in a stagnant bog. This is the world when it was 'without form and void'. Here you feel that God never 'moved upon the face of the waters'. Nothing has ever moved here except evil. Shakespeare was born in the blessed coloured counties of the fertile land of Stratford: Hardy here with this desolation always reaching over his shoulder. No man can understand Hardy who has not been lost on the heath at night.

Ralph Wightman (The Wessex Heathland, 1953)

Riding Across the Heath 1782

By seven o'clock I was on horseback; and [leaving Ringwood] cross'd much bleak, heathy country, till near Longham, where I pass'd an handsome river over a long stone bridge. The road then continues over the same dreary country.

Hon. John Byng (later 5th Viscount Torrington)

Riding Across the Heath 1795

From Christchurch we proceeded on horseback to Poole. After going about two miles on the high road, we turned off by the advice of a farmer, who told us we should find a much shorter way by going to the left, which, however, came to the top of a high cliff, where we could not find the least track of road. We were, however, recompensed in some degree by a most delightful view of the sea.

After enjoying this noble scene, we turned our horses' heads and rode in the direction of Poole, as we thought, for on this barren and uncultivated heath there was not a human being to direct us.

Diary of the Duke of Rutland (1795)

Parson's Pleasure

A conifer plantation on the heath in the vicinity of Morden Bog is named 'Parson's Pleasure' for a reason which is explained to the passer-by on a commemorative plaque, as follows –

This experiment was designed by Frank Parsons MBE, Chief Forester at Wareham from 1950 to 1968. The water-logged heath in this area is one of the worst sites in Europe. The experiment demonstrates a practical way of making it plantable by mechanical drainage and fertilising.

He died in 1968 and this plot is dedicated to his memory.

A Farmer's View

There are very few heath farmers in Dorset. There are a few heath dwellers but they are not farmers in the sense that a Forester is a farmer. In *The Return of the Native* Thomas Hardy describes the besom-maker and the furzecutter who were heath men, but most of the characters in the novel had jobs on the good land of the river valleys. This was sound observation. A few men took what little bounty the heath afforded, furze, firewood and peat.

A few men dug clay, and kept an odd pony on the heath for their convenience, but there has never been any farming in the real sense of the word. Many landowners have tried reclamation. Here and there the banks of their old fences can still be seen. Many attempts have been made at afforestation, including recent new plantations of sombre firs. Possibly the Forestry Commission's new woods will succeed. The Commission have the advantage of scientific knowledge of soils and the use of modern tools. So far, though, the heath has always won in the end when a man has tried to get a living from it. The hungry soil needs perpetual feeding with dung, lime and chemicals to grow crops. Even then it seems to take a malignant pleasure in growing annual weeds. Seedling nettles, spurrey and corn marigolds come up in thick carpets which smother the poor tame vegetables. As a scientist I know that there is not anything really malignant about a soil. There are no Spirits of the Waste trying to hold their own dreary land. This light sand when it is cultivated and manured makes a perfect seed-bed for tiny annual weeds and they come up in their millions. That is all.

Ralph Wightman (The Wessex Heathland, 1953)

The Great Heath

The Great Heath, when surveyed as a whole, is a haphazard tract of sand covered with heather, bracken, and gorse, presenting highlands and lowlands, bald hills and dry, corroded glens. In some places life is so hard as to be nigh to starvation, while elsewhere are comfortable thickets of pines and firs, or green hollows where the rain has dribbled into pools. The largest of these pools, the "Old Decoy Pond," is a patch of blue in the waste where wild ducks are tempted to rest for a while on their voyagings. Elsewhere the water has collected into sour swamps or shivering bogs.

The general aspect of the wild is morose and inhospitable, shrivelled with thirst, beaten and blown by the wind, and parched by the sun. It was into such a tract as this that the scapegoat was driven to wander until it died. It would seem as if a shadow rested on this homeless country, serving to make brighter the meadows and cornfields around it. As Thomas Hardy says, "The face of the heath by its mere complexion adds half an hour to evening: it can, in like manner, retard the dawn, sadden noon, anticipate the frowning of storms, scarcely generated, and intensify the opacity of a moonless midnight to a cause of shaking and dread."

The tone of the moor is a russet-brown, splashed by the bracken with green and by the heather with purple. Under the summer sun marvellous colours appear, which break, as the clouds ride over, into infinite modulations. A far-away plateau may be Gobelin blue, and a near hillock bronze-brown. There may be here a bare slope of mushroom-coloured sand, and there a reedy marsh of parrot-green.

Beyond the burial mounds and the few buff roads which are hurrying across the waste, there is no sign of human interest on the Heath except this – one knoll, drab as a cinder-heap, stands up against the sky-line, and on its summit are three gaunt pines with outstretched arms, bared by the wind, which might be the three crosses on Calvary.

The Great Heath is a veritable part of that Britain the Celts knew, since upon its untameable surface twenty centuries have wrought no change. It is a primitive country still. The wheat, the orchard trees, and the garden flowers on its confines are products of civilisation, and are newcomers to the land. Here, still living, are the rough, hardy aborigines – the heather, the bracken, and the gorse.

Frederick Treves (Highways and Byways in Dorset, 1906)

7 · TOWN AND VILLAGE

The place-names of Dorset are a source of delight to the collectors of such items – and to no-one more than to John Betjeman. He found a poet's music in them and went on, for a lark, to decorate the headstones in Thomas Hardy's village churchyard with the euphonious names of some of the celebrities of the 'Thirties. Before him, Frederick Treves had mused on the same subject, starting with Toller Porcorum in the days when it had a railway station.

The county town, Dorchester, will be most familiar to readers in its description by Thomas Hardy in The Mayor of Casterbridge. *An earlier description comes from John Byng, Viscount Torrington in 1782, and a later one from Treves in 1906: both are particularly impressed by the tree-lined Walks. In Sherborne it is the multiplicity of architectural styles which wins a lyrical tribute from H.J. Massingham.*

Throughout the county it is the long perspective of its history that gives depth of character to town and village – and eminently so in the archaic language of John Leland as he wrote down his impression of the remarkable complex of Badbury Rings, Wimborne Minster and Kingston Lacy, reminding us of the seamless continuity that links the Iron Age fortbuilders to the Roman road-surveyor, the medieval monk and the Victorian art-connoisseur.

In a lighter vein Harriette Wilson, the celebrated courtesan who inspired the Duke of Wellington's 'Publish and be damn'd,' contributes her account of Charmouth and Lyme Regis when she fled from London on the Exeter mail-coach and was not quite sure whether she ended up in Dorset or Devon.

Outstanding in rural Dorset are Cerne Abbas and Ashmore. Those who know only the highly desirable residential quality of Cerne today will scarcely recognise the dereliction which followed the replacement of stage-coach by railway. Ashmore, by contrast, has preserved a settlement round its mysterious pond for a couple of thousand years without the benefit of turnpike road, coach, railroad or helicopter.

With the dignity of a rearguard Shaftesbury concludes this chapter, to the accompaniment of village bells.

Dorset

Rime Intrinsica, Fontmell Magna, Sturminster Newton and Melbury Bubb,
Whist upon whist upon whist upon whist drive, in Institute, Legion and Social Club.
Horny hands that hold the aces which this morning held the plough –
While Tranter Reuben, T.S. Eliot, H.G. Wells and Edith Sitwell lie in Mellstock Churchyard now.

Lord's Day bells from Bingham's Melcombe, Iwerne Minster, Shroton, Plush,
Down the grass between the beeches, mellow in the evening hush.
Gloved hands that hold the hymn-book, which this morning milked the cow –
While Tranter Reuben, Mary Borden, Brian Howard and Harold Acton lie in Mellstock Churchyard now.

Light's abode, celestial Salem! Lamps of evening, smelling strong,
Gleaming on the pitch-pine, waiting, almost empty evensong:
From the aisles each window smiles on grave and grass and yew-tree bough –
While Tranter Reuben, Gordon Selfridge, Edna Best and Thomas Hardy lie in Mellstock Churchyard now.

John Betjeman (Collected Poems, 1958)

Place-Names

Toller Porcorum is a convenient centre from whence to visit certain of the midlands of Dorset. There is a station there, although it has dropped the cognomen of Porcorum. The name is peculiar, but of remarkable names of places this Toller is by no means the only example in the county. We have, on this side of Dorset, Whitchurch Canonicorum and Ryme Intrinseca. We have also in the county the Wriggle River and the Devil's Brook, God's Blessing Green and Giddy Green, Grammar's Hill and Mount Ararat, Hungry Down and Dancing Hill. The names of certain farms and holdings are possibly more curious still. There is something of the forlorn hope about Ratcombe Barn, Wooden Cabbage Farm and Labour-in-Vain. Starvington Farm, Poor Lot, and Charity Bottom are not attractive titles for those who have property to sell. Botany Bay Barn and Menagerie have no doubt a story, while there is the sarcasm of utter isolation about Bedlam, Marshalsea, and Bridewell.

Frederick Treves (Highways and Byways in Dorset, 1906)

Dorchester in 1782

Dorchester reminds me of a foreign town, for the approaches are planted and there is a shady walk round the town on the old ramparts. The gaol fronts the street, and is a nuisance to passengers; I was told that the felons were let out to harvest-work.

Hon. John Byng (later 5th Viscount Torrington)

Dorchester in 1906

One of the most beautiful features of Dorchester is it ceinture of green, for on three sides it is surrounded by avenues of trees – of sycamores, limes, and chestnuts. On the fourth side runs the River Frome through reedy meadows. These avenues, called 'The Walks', were planted between 1700 and 1712 on the lines of the ancient walls. Until quite recent years the Walks formed the outermost boundaries of the town, beyond which no house ventured to stray. The town indeed, as I recollect it, was still 'huddled all together, and shut in by a square wall of trees, like a plot of garden ground by box-edging', as a character in one of Hardy's novels observes. These formal avenues or boulevards give to Dorchester an uncommon air and a little of the aspect of a foreign town. The principal roads, too, which approach the capital enter it with great solemnity through avenues of fine trees.

The best view of the town is from the top of the West Street. From this height the town slopes downhill to the river. There is a long, straight, yellow road, with a line of irregularly disposed houses on either side of it. No two are of quite the same height. They favour white walls, ample roofs, bow windows, and stone porticoes. Where there are shops there are patches of bright colour, striped sun-blinds, and a posse of carriers' carts. Over the house-tops rise the stolid tower of St Peter's, the clock turret, and the pale spire of All Saints' Church. Then, at the far-away foot of the slope, the diminished road can be seen running out into the green water meads, to be finally lost among the trees of Stinsford.

Frederick Treves (Highways and Byways in Dorset, 1906)

Wimborne, Badbury Rings and Kingston Lacy

The toun of Winburn is yet meatly good and reasonably welle inhabitid, it hath beene a very large thing, and was in price in tyme of the West-Saxon kinges.

There be in and about it diverse chapelles that in tymes paste were, as I have lernid, paroche chirchis of the very toun of Winburne.

The Saxon kinges had hard by the toun a castelle now caullid Babyri [Badbury] but clerely down. The diches, hilles, and site therof be yet evidently seene, now conyes borough in it.

There hath beene sins a fair maner place caullid Kingeston-Haul, and this is also now in a maner clerely defacid. It berith in wrytinges the name of Kingeston Lascy [Kingston Lacy]. Whereapon I gather that one of the Lacys, predecessors onto Henry Lascy Erle of Lincoln, buildid this house, and I gather therby also, that the Lascys were lordes of Winburne, and by hym it cam to John of Gaunt Duke of Lancastre, to the which duke [dom] it yet longgith. And the courtes for Winburn be yet kept at Kingeston.

John Leland (1535-43)

Charmouth and Lyme Regis

Charmouth, Devonshire [sic]

My dearest Sister

It was a beautiful May evening when the mail-coach set us down at a little country-looking sort of pot-house in this village. I was wretchedly oppressed by melancholy and fatigue. I inquired for beds, and was informed by very good luck that my landlady's only bedroom, containing two small, neat, white beds, was at our disposal. The stair-case was a ladder, or rather a ladder was the stair-case. We will not be particular. I was soon in bed, and my maid contrived to procure me a cup of tea, which is all I remember happening to me till about eight the next morning, when the broad sun, shining in my face for want of window curtains, induced me to rise. As for my maid, she was already dressed and busy with my trunks, searching out my clean linen.

As soon as I was dressed, my good-natured landlady begged I would come down to breakfast, while it was hot. She gave us most excellent Devonshire cream and hot Devonshire cakes. In short, everything was so clean and delicious in its way, that it was difficult not to be hungry. After our breakfast we inquired for a guide to show us some of the beauties of that part of the country. 'My little boy will take you over to Lyme Regis. He is particularly cute, and can tell you more than I can,' said the good landlady. 'What distance is Lyme Regis from this village?' I inquired. 'Oh laws! only about two miles, and the most beautifullest walk in the world.'

Behold us then, on our road to Lyme Regis, with a little cute Devonshire lad for our guide. Lyme Regis is a sort of Brighton in miniature, all bustle and confusion, assembly-rooms, donkey-riding, raffling, etc., etc. It was sixpence per night to attend the assemblies, and much cheaper if paid by the season. We went to a little inn and dined. From the window, I was much amused to see the number of smart old maids that were tripping down the streets, in turbans or artificial flowers twined around their wigs, on the light fantastic toe, to the sixpenny assembly-rooms at five in the evening! They were very pleasantly situated near the sea, and as we walked past their windows we saw them all drinking tea and playing cards. There were amongst them persons of the highest rank; but the society was chiefly composed of people of very small independent fortunes, who for economy had settled at Lyme Regis; or of such as required sea-bathing; natives, either of Exeter or any neighbouring town.

There were plenty of furnished lodgings to be let at Lyme Regis; but I determined if possible to establish myself at Charmouth, that place being so much more to my taste. At eight o'clock in the evening we arrived at our humble inn at Charmouth in a donkey-cart, and immediately retired to rest. At six the next morning, since the broad daylight would not suffer me to sleep, I determined to walk all about the village in search of lodgings, before I could be induced to give up the hopes of securing a residence there. We found no difficulty in procuring the same excellent breakfast, which was served up with perfect neatness by half-past six, and at a little after seven the gay and fashionable Harriette Wilson was to be seen strolling about the little village of Charmouth at though it had been her native place, and she had never heard tell of the pomps and vanities of this very wicked world.

We carefully examined every house we passed for a bill indicative of lodgings to let; but in vain. They all appeared to be inhabited by some respectable individual, neither rich nor poor. We had walked twice through the village and round about it, and were bending our steps towards our little pot-house in mute despair, when my attention was arrested by the striking loveliness of a young lady who was watering some flowers at one of the windows of a house I had before admired for its peculiar neatness. She smiled so very graciously that I was encouraged in my wish to address her. The moment she saw me make towards the little street-door, she ran and opened it herself. After many apologies, I entreated to be informed if I was likely to succeed in obtaining board and lodging with any private family at Charmouth. The young lady entreated me to walk into the parlour and sit down, like people who had taken a liking to each other, and then she left me to speak to her mother on the subject of procuring me a comfortable residence. In a very short time she returned, and presented me to two very respectable-looking women in deep mourning, as her mother and aunt. After a little more conversation, Mrs. Edmond, which was the name of the young lady's mother, spoke to me to this effect: 'I am the widow of an officer in the navy, whose death, when abroad, I learned ten years ago from a brother-officer who had been present, and came here to convey his last requests to his family; since that moment, having for ever renounced the world, I live only in my child, and have nothing to do on earth but to attend to and promote her happiness. She feels greatly disposed to benefit by your pleasant society, and has made it her anxious request that I will offer you an asylum in my house: therefore, if you like to inhabit a snug room which faces the country, it is at your service, and you may keep it entirely for your own use. I have also a servant's room for your maid, and, if you can accustom yourself to our family dinner, the thing is arranged at once.'

Everything, which the warmest affection or the oldest friendship could have dictated, was put in practice for our comfort and accommodation. I had a nice bedroom, adjoining the snug little sitting-room where I am now writing, and Mrs. Edmond, who has long studied the qualities of medicine, in order to render herself useful to the poor people about the village, insisted on doctoring me, declaring that I was feverish. One of the ladies rubbed my feet, another administered white wine-whey, and another – but I have swelled in my letter to such an enormous length, that I must defer saying any more about these good people till my next.

Your most affectionate sister,

H.W.

Harriette Wilson (Memoirs, c. 1815-20)

Cerne Abbas in 1906

The town of Cerne Abbas, when viewed from the Dorchester road, is a cosy settlement tucked away in an amphitheatre of sage-green hills. There are many trees in the town, so that, compared with the poor bare downs that close it in, it looks warm and comfortable, and curled up like a dormouse in a sunny corner.

On entering the main street of Cerne it is evident that some trouble has fallen upon the Abbey itself. It is silent and well-nigh deserted. Sad to tell, Cerne Abbas is dying, and has already fallen into a state of hebetude. The joy went out of its life when the Abbey was taken away. The inhabitants in their affliction tried to make of the place a manufacturing town. They made boots, and no doubt made them well. They made beer, and became for a time famous. They developed a market. They took to smuggling, and met for a time with most encouraging success. Nothing, however, went well for long in Cerne after the last monk slinked out of the Abbey. One enterprise failed after another. There was still the great high-road left with its coaches, for Cerne was a comfortable stage from Dorchester. When railways made their brutal advance into Dorset the heart of Cerne gave way utterly; the coaches ceased one by one, and from that moment Cerne Abbas has never smiled again.

It is a clean, trim, old-world town, which has remained unchanged for Heaven knows how many years. Its streets are quaint and picturesque, for they all belong to the England of the coaching times. No two houses are alike; some are tiled, some thatched, some roofed with stone. In not a few of them the first floor overhangs the causeway, according to a forgotten fashion. The place, however, is empty and decaying and strangely silent. Grass is growing in the streets; many houses have been long deserted, many have their windows boarded up, or are falling into listless ruin. Here are empty barns, gates falling off their hinges, and doorways grown up with weeds. There are quaint old shops with bow windows, but the windows are empty of everything but a faded red curtain, while over the door, in very dim paint, are traces of a name. One feels compelled to walk very quietly through the echoing streets, and to talk in whispers, for fear that the sleep of Cerne should be broken.

So sleepy and indifferent has Cerne become that it has even neglected its Giant. This colossal human form is carved on the slope of one of the barren hills which surround the town. The figure is of great antiquity, and dates – so the learned say – from pre-Roman times. Of its history and its purpose nothing is known. The Giant is a fine figure of a man, for he stands 180 feet in height; the length of each of his fingers is seven feet, and the length of the club he wields is 120 feet. Cerne Abbas the Depressed has so long ceased to care for its Giant that the poor Goliath has become grown over with grass, and is nearly invisible to the eye.

Frederick Treves (Highways and Byways in Dorset, 1906)

East Melbury and Ashmore

The road out of East Melbury leads past the old dew-pond which Melbury boys once turned into a cycle track, to the hill road known as the Zig-Zag. This is a beautiful piece of engineering which takes the gradient to the top of the down in five hairpin bends, the drop below is screened by young beeches. At the top, the road emerges from its green vaulting to come out above Melbury Bottom with a long view down towards Melbury Abbas. In the other direction the church towers of Shaftesbury can be made out against the sky on the long, dark sandstone ridge. On the horizon is King Alfred's Tower and ahead is the Ox Drove and the beginning of the Chase.

Ashmore is the first village up here and the highest in Dorset. As the road forks for Ashmore, at its highest point there is a neolithic long barrow just beside it, half hidden by the growth of the hedge bank. Standing on the great burial mound one can see across the whole cloud-patterned expanse of the Chase, over the New Forest to the Solent and the white cliffs of the Isle of Wight beyond. On a clear day the view is quite outstanding, and in all those miles not one town is visible. If they exist they hide themselves completely. Indeed the only one in direct line of vision is Ringwood, and that is lost beyond the Forest. Ashmore, down a gentle, unfrequented lane is almost entirely unspoiled. The lane ends at a pond, and almost in it, a round, deep pond complete with ducks and geese. The school, church and houses gather round the pond like some old engraving. Near the church are two delightful, yet modest, seventeenth-century houses. The village retains also the traditional junketing known as the "Filleigh Loo", with country dancing and festivities, the "band" being set on a wagon out in the pond. The nearest place of refreshment was for long at Tollard Royal in the next county, and the road round there was long and hilly; but there was a short cut known as the "muddy track" which came out by Tollard Green. For long the people of Ashmore petitioned that this "muddy track" might be made into a hard road for their greater ease and convenience. When the powers-that-be turned a deaf ear they started a subscription for the work themselves. I was present at the ceremonial opening in the early 1950's when a "muck-spreader" went before, but instead of sowing manure far and wide, it cast out wild flowers – poppies, thunder daisies, and scabious – picked for the occasion. The highest, loneliest village in Dorset is not without its moments of glory.

Monica Hutchings (Inside Dorset, 1965)

Shaftesbury

At Shaftesbury, as at many another Dorset town, the dweller in cities can see something of the charm of the life of little towns. There is a curious absence of traffic in the streets, and a sense that the place is deserted.

Everyone walks in the road, and from the tramp of their feet on the crisp way it would seem that shoes here are of heavier make than in cities. In London the passing crowd is dumb, for all are strangers. Here each knows the other, so that scarcely a soul goes by without a word of greeting. The boys in the streets are whistling a tune which was popular two years ago: many people stand at street corners, as if waiting for someone who never comes: most of the men carry sticks, and most of the women baskets.

There is a personality about the place which is lacking in those great cities which never slumber nor sleep. In the morning the town wakes up. The householder opens his front door and stands out in the road in his shirt-sleeves to appraise the weather. The idle apprentice takes down the shop shutters, and – between intervals of gossip – places buckets, spades, tubs, horse-collars, and other goods, according to their kinds, upon the edge of the pavement. The sexton strolls by to toll the morning bell. A leisurely man drags a drowsy horse to the blacksmith's to be shod, and in a while there is the sound of a hammer on an anvil. A passing gig, that started from some farmhouse at sunrise, interests the waking town. It may carry a dairymaid on her way to a new situation, a couple of milk cans, or a confused heifer under a net.

A man proceeds to sweep the road with a besom made of a bundle of twigs according to the pattern of centuries ago. He shows a willingness to converse with everyone – man, woman, or child – who will stop to "pass the time of day with him." As something of an event a miller's cart, with a team of four fine horses, climbs up the High Street. They may have come so far that they appear to be foreign. There is always a vain, boastful dog with the waggon, who clamours that the town should stir to see his horses, his wain, his waggoner, and his sacks, all of which he regards as of unequalled magnificence.

In the evening the town goes lazily to sleep. The yawning shops close reluctantly, the long shadows of the setting sun fall across the drowsy street. The children have vanished. The lovers have come back from the lanes arm in arm. A tired dog is asleep in the centre of the road. Lights go out in the windows one by one, until the place is silent and dark. The visitor from the city falls asleep, lulled by the unwonted odour of a blown out candle and of a pillow that has been embalmed in lavender. Possibly about midnight a single horseman trots into the sleeping town, and in a while two horsemen clatter out again along the same road. From which it may be known that an anxious man has come in from the country to fetch the doctor, and is taking him back as if by the bidding of some Habeas Corpus.

Frederick Treves, 1906

Lydlinch Bells

When skies wer peäle wi' twinklen stars,
An' whislen aïr a-risèn keen;
An' birds did leäve the icy bars
To vind, in woods, their mossy screen;
When vrozen grass, so white's a sheet,
Did scrunchy sharp below our veet,
An' water, that did sparkle red
At zunzet, were a-vrozen dead;
The ringers then did spend an hour
A-ringen changes up in tow'r;
Vor Lydlinch bells be good vor sound,
An' liked by all the naighbours round.

An' while along the leafless boughs
O' ruslen hedges, win's did pass,
An' orts ov haÿ, a-left by cows,
Did russle on the vrozen grass,
An' maidens' pails, wi' all their work
A-done, did hang upon their vurk,
An' they, avore the fleäman brand,
Did teäke their needle-work in hand,
The men did cheer their heart an hour,
A-ringen changes up in tow'r;

Vor Lydlinch bells be good vor sound,
An' liked by all the naighbours round.

Their sons did pull the bells that rung
Their mothers' wedden peals avore,
The while their fathers led em young
An' blushen vrom the churches door,
An' still did cheem, wi' happy sound,
As time did bring the Zundays round,
An' call em to the holy pleäce
Vor heav'nly gifts o' peace an' greäce;
An' vo'k did come, a-streamen slow
Along below the trees in row,
While they, in merry peals, did sound
The bells vor all the naighbours round.

An' when the bells, wi' changen peal,
Did smite their own vo'k's window-peänes,
Their sof'en'd sound did often steal
Wi' west winds drough the Bagber leänes;
Or, as the win' did shift, mid goo
Where woody Stock do nessle lew,
Or where the risen moon did light
The walls o' Thornhill on the height;
An' zoo, whatever time mid bring
To meäke their vive clear vaices zing,
Still Lydlinch bells wer good vor sound,
An' liked by all the naighbours round.

William Barnes (1801-1886)

8 · DOWNLAND

Not everyone appreciates downland. T.H. Huxley, for instance, saw in it nothing more than 'a mutton-suggesting prettiness'. Newcomers to Dorset were sometimes alarmed, as Surtees was, by the featureless spaciousness of these rolling landscapes in which it was easy to lose all sense of direction; yet it is that very freedom to roam in the tonic freshness of downland air which can be so exhilarating.

No-one could have loved the Dorset Downs more than H.J. Massingham. To walk them in imagination with him as one's companion and guide is an experience to cherish.

Open Country

So much of Dorset is downland that less than a hundred years ago it was possible for those who knew how to avoid bogs to make across the unfenced country without using the roads at all. The carters would hitch four horses on to a two horse load and go right across country from Dorchester to Salisbury, taking several days about it, but often not being on any sort of road. Thus all tolls were avoided.

Dorset Up Along and Down Along, 1935

Dorsetshire Milestones

Of all the countries I have ever been in, Dorsetshire is the most difficult for a stranger to find his way about. Fingerposts there are none;

downs, with their 'Dorsetshire milestones,' stretch about in all directions, and the cross-roads, over the bleak and barren heaths, are puzzling beyond description.

[Note: Travelling to Bloxworth House Surtees left the Weymouth coach at Blandford and travelled on in a yellow post-chaise.]

We were soon passing through divers fields, commons and opens, and winding about the tortuous by-roads which all countrymen delight to follow until I found myself on a trackless open down. To my anxious enquiry the postboy replied – 'it be all right – these be Bloxworth Downs and the House be just over the hill before us; these 'ere white heaps you zee marks the road – they be what we calls Dorzetshire mileztones'.

I looked out of the window on the right, and by the light of the moon, which gleamed dimly through the passing clouds, I saw small heaps of chalk, laid at intervals of five or six yards apart, which, contrasting with the dark sward of the turf, pointed out the line and guided us over the downs, bringing us ultimately to the door of Bloxworth House.

'Yorkshireman' (R. S. Surtees) c.1835

The Chalk Downs of Dorset

The vertebral column which crosses Dorset from the Stour and separates the oak-dressed Vale of Blackmore from the southern lands of the coast leaves the archaeologist except at moments rather cold. But it makes the geographer's pulse beat faster. What is happening to the chalk? Follow the range above Durweston by Shillingstone and Okeford Hills, along the green track over Bell Hill and above the wooded crescent of Woolland Hill to Bulbarrow. It is a difficult road to trace, because, though the southwestern track of the Great Ridgeway from Avebury pursues this route through mid-Dorset, it is by a series of broken ribbons. For once in a way, the chalk traveller feels more at home along the twisty lanes of the valley through Ibberton, gay with orange walls and brown thatch, than with the abrupt hill-masses rapidly changing shape as he moves. A queer word to use for the downs – abrupt – and the reverse of what Gilbert White felt about them. But these downs are different. If Cranborne Chase is half in and half out of Salisbury Plain, this range still farther to the west is a prodigal son. It has lost the large tranquillity of Wiltshire, the beautiful assonance of line that belongs to the mother-land of the chalk. The slopes are acute, not merely steep; the valleys are over-shadowed, not gently let in to the hills swelling away from them. Sharp cols and narrow passes break up the continuity of the ridge, and tongues of land ram their way outwards, lacking the monumental sweep of the Wiltshire spurs. The landscape is disturbed; conflict and struggle are written over it in uneven lettering. And this is actually so. As the heavy woods and bracken wastes and hairy covering reveal, the chalk as it flows westward towards the Devon frontier is meeting the crumpled lias of county Devon, and the shock of the encounter is bearing down the spacious manner of the downs.

Yet suddenly, on Bulbarrow, the archaic concord is recaptured. Not on the back of the shaggy giant itself, dark with furze, tossing with foxglove, willow-herb and ragwort, rude with matted bushes and dishevelled hedgerows, but in what lies immediately below. To the north, the Somerset flats join the rich, blue claylands of Blackmore Vale and to the south – for here the range swings southward – the broken outlines are still more visible, while the green valley that belongs to Milton Abbey throws a wedge across the passage of the uplands towards Dorchester. The flying buttresses of this Abbey, like those of the pinnacled, honey-coloured tower of Piddletrenthide, one of the loveliest in Dorset, perfectly translate into stone the grassy spurs of downland. What restores the downland sense is the little camp of Rawlsbury whose rings, directly below you, encircle their smooth green hill with all that music of motion in repose which expresses the genius of the chalk. Bulbarrow (and it has its dilapidated round barrow) has the splendour of sheer uncouth wildness, but Rawlsbury's is the art of quieter downs.

The highland way continues over Nettlecombe Tout and wooded Church Hill above Piddletrenthide and Piddlehinton, and so to the region of the Minternes above Cerne Abbas. The chalk loses more and more control over the shapes of its hills until once more, at Cerne, its naked serenity is restored. Cerne Abbas itself is exceptional among Dorset chalk villages; it is partly Tudor in style, as the big houses of Cranborne Chase tend, Crichel, for instance, to be Palladian. It is unusually lavish in half-timbering, while the combination of black flints with light stone, gables with bow windows, reminds you of the best village architecture of Wiltshire. Behind the village and above the Abbey gateway, the famous Giant is carved out of the turf, almost upright for his one hundred and eighty feet of length upon the almost precipitous bare slope.

The range south of Cerne goes on towards the border with a gusto, a fantasia of forms incredibly chalk. Knowledge, not observation, tells you that this jumble of hills, crowding onward in disorder, with flat tops and conical sides, with toy peaks and gorges, with tops covered in oak and bracken and gorse and highly spectacular, is still chalk. But it is, though weakening, right away from Minterne Magna past High Stoy, over Batcombe Common and by Evershot to Toller Down Gate, two miles from Beaminster, squatting below and beloved of the west country poet, William Barnes. But the downland race is run to the west, and Beaminster Down is only an outlier, that stops dead and looks at the foreign greensand of Pilsdon Pen and Lewesdon and Lambert's Castle, which carry the Great Ridgeway yet nearer to the Devon sea. Beaminster sees also the limestone uplands of Mendip to the north-west, but I turn with the wide curve of the chalk above Maiden Newton into the spell of Dorchester.

A kind of spell it is. No sooner have I climbed the rounded steep of Eggardon and turned my head to follow the mighty crescent of hills from Long and Little Bredy to Abbotsbury and Upway, south of Dorchester, than I find myself once more among familiar scenes of ridge and slope and headland and spur, composed as ever and united in an unbroken sweep towards the east. There could not be a greater contrast from the country around Powerstock, two miles to the west of Eggardon Camp, where the roads slice gashes through a motley of hills with shapes both of comedy and strife. Yet Eggardon itself, both hill and hill-town, is in the classic style of downland and makes, in the union of them both, one of the noblest bluffs over the entire area of the chalk. Pits and lynchets of the Celtic village lie scattered over its plateau within ramparts so lofty that you can eat your lunch (as I have done) in the outer ditch with no more than a zephyr straying to your cheeks from the gale overhead. Eggardon is an outpost of the chalk from the south, but as you walk the berm of its most massive rampart round the whole oblong, you gather into your experience the Cleopatra-like variations of this unique West Country – tumbled dark-haired Devon far to the south-west, the sombre limestone ranges beyond Yeovil to the north, the mid-Dorset backbone to the north-east, chalk but tipsily compounded with other soils, and south to the sea this fair world of the true, the open downs. The south-eastern spur of Eggardon tapers down towards them and thither is my way.

Yet there is a difference which distinguishes Dorset's southern chalk from any of the sky-wedded downlands of my journey thus far, and it is a difference which, I think, grants to southern Dorset from Swyre Head to Ballard Down above Studland the supremacy in beauty over all the chalklands. In the first place, the ridges are accompanied for their whole length into the Purbeck Hills by a coast-line unmatched, in my opinion, by any other littoral in England, even the Cornish and North Devonian. Often the downs, as by Florusbury, the white cliffs east of Weymouth, Chaldon Down, Hanbury Tout, Bindon Hill, the Arish Mell Gap and Worbarrow, and again at their eastern termination on Ballard Down, themselves shape that coast-line. But they share it with other formations, with the curved scimitar of the Chesil Beach, the grim rugged oolitic mass of Portland, the pliable walls of the Kimmeridge shale, with the sternly castellated limestone of St Aldhelm's Head, with blown sand, alluvium and wealden. The result is a coast of wild and yet subtle contours, of delicacy passing into magnificence of form, barren and raw and a paint-box of colour. It seems as though hallowed relics of all the bones that make up England's multiform anatomy had been piously collected and laid there. But not indiscriminately, for each stratum has its place and due prominence and contributes to the transcendental harmony of the whole. And this is just what you notice along the downland range itself, whether on or a little removed from the sea. The chalk is not mixed up with other strata as it is along the mid-Dorset range to a width of ten miles. The Purbeck, Kimmeridge, Oolite and Bagshot Beds are its neighbours, while at the same time the plain chalk is dominant enough to achieve that continuity of line which is its natural development.

Thus, over the area of the six Winterbornes between Little Bredy and Broadmayne, the outcrops of oak and heath, the saurian snout of Portland, the dark hump of Blackdown, do not bind the grace of Chalbury Camp, airily swinging its oval out towards the sea, nor interrupt the sweep of White Horse Hill to the gap at Poxwell. When the large-mannered downs reach Purbeck, they narrow to a thin hog's

back with the night-shaded wastes of Egdon rolling against their shore.
But their definition and identity are not lost, as they are along the
parallel ribbing of the mid-Dorset range southward from its northern
scarp, where the waves of cornland submerge the downland characters
beneath their golden surge. Deep woods are the skirting of Lulworth Castle, but they keep their distance without obscuring the long
profile of the downs and Florusbury or Flowers Barrow Camp rising
enchanted from the sea. I neared journey's end, Nine Barrow, with
only Creech Down and Ballard Head to come. To the right lay
the steep of Broad Bench beyond Brandy Bay, and before me was
Povington Hill and the smooth but pyramidal head of Creech Barrow.
To the left Egdon, Poole and the Little Sea were like the world of
Genesis, but just emerged from chaos. South of Brownsea Island and
the Studland sands one white sail like an apparition rode the drowsing
sea. Space, form and colour were celestially one. Into this synthesis the
chalk passes in the last act of its Dorset journey.

H.J. Massingham (The English Downland, 1936)

9 · VISITORS

The literary travellers, whose accounts of their journeys into the west country illuminate the English scene from Queen Elizabeth's days to Queen Victoria's, were seldom drawn into rural Dorset. They described the special features of the coast – Brownsea island, Weymouth, Lyme Regis – but more often their route beyond Salisbury turned to Stonehenge, the city of Bath, Glastonbury and Wookey Hole. As late as 1890 Roger North's first impression of Dorset was of novelty and strangeness where people spoke in an odd way.

Sir Joseph Banks came to visit an aunt at Tarrant Gunville and took the opportunity to call at Kingston Lacy. John Wesley came to preach at Shaftesbury, and other visitors were drawn to visit Dorset's famous poets. William Allingham, the Irish poet, came as a visiting neighbour since he was a Customs Officer at Lymington. He brought his friend Alfred, Lord Tennyson, to visit William Barnes on their way to Lyme Regis. Francis Kilvert was an earlier admirer, paying tribute to Barnes. Edward VIII as Prince of Wales was entertained at Max Gate by Hardy, to the satirical delight of Max Beerbohm; Wordsworth came for a short stay at Racedown; and Rupert Brooke lost his way to the Fleur de Lys in Cranborne.

Coming into Dorsetshire

The counties near London, as Hampshire and part of Wiltshire, have little singular to be noted, either of strangeness of situation or character of the people, more than ordinary; but coming into Dorsetshire, the country grows new, and things looked a little strange; the people spoke oddly, and the women wore white mantles which they call whittells. And the houses were of stone and slate; and what we call gentility of everything began to wear off.

Roger North (The Lives of the Norths, 1890)

John Wesley at Shaftesbury

At five I preached in Bridgewater to a well-behaved company, and then rode on to Middlesey.

We rode from hence to Shaftesbury, where I preached, between six and seven, to a serious and quiet congregation. We had another happy opportunity at five in the morning, when abundance of people were present ... Soon after I was sat down, a Constable came and said, "Sir, the Mayor discharges you from preaching in this Borough any more." I replied, "While King George gives me leave to preach, I shall not ask leave of the Mayor of Shaftesbury."

John Wesley (Journal)

A Visit to Kingston Lacy 1767

Went this morn to Kinston Hall in the Vale of Winbourne, to see Mr Banks, my namesake, an old Bachelor of 70 and more. His house is an exceeding good one, but quite of the last age, as there is not one sash in the whole. Its furniture, however, of Pictures is very Capital; a Collection of Sr Peter Lellys portraits very fine; two Spanish boys eating fruit by Morellio [Murillo], a Landscape by Bergem, a copy or original of Rembrants Rabbi. But four pictures are Remarkably Capital, perhaps Guido: they represent Pope Gregory the Great, the Great St Augustine and two more of the fathers: but Mr Banks has no Catalogue and knows very little about them.

Sir Joseph Banks (1767)

A Luncheon

In 1923 Edward, Prince of Wales, visited Dorchester and had lunch at Thomas Hardy's home, Max Gate.

Lift latch, step in, be welcome, Sir,
Albeit to see you I'm unglad
And your face is fraught with a deathly shyness
Bleaching what pink it may have had.
Come in, come in, Your Royal Highness.

Beautiful weather? – Sir, that's true,
Though the farmers are casting rueful looks
At tilth's and pasture's dearth of spryness
Yes, Sir, I've written several books. –
A little more chicken, your Royal Highness?

Lift latch, step out, your car is there,
To bear you hence from this antient vale.
We are both of us aged by our strange brief nighness
But each of us lives to tell the tale.
Farewell, farewell, Your Royal Highness.

Sir Max Beerbohm (1923)

A Visit to William Barnes

Thursday, May Eve, 1874 – To-day I visited and made the acquaintance and I hope the friendship of William Barnes, the great idyllic Poet of England. Up at 6 o'clock, breakfast at 6.30, and left Chippenham by the 7.15 train.

Mr Henry Moule, the Vicar of Fordington for nearly half a century, met me at the Dorchester Station [and] we walked together to the Poet's house, Winterbourne Came Rectory, about a mile from Fordington. The house lies a little back from the glaring white high road and stands on a lawn fringed with trees. It is thatched and a thatched verandah runs along its front. As we turned in at the iron gates from the high road and went down the gravel path the poet was walking in

the verandah. He welcomed us cordially and brought us into his drawing room on the right-hand side of the door. He is an old man, over
seventy, rather bowed with age, but apparently hale and strong. 'Excuse my study gown,' he said. He wore a dark grey loose gown girt
round the waist with a black cord and tassle, black knee breeches,
black silk stockings and gold buckled shoes.

I was immediately struck by the beauty and grandeur of his head. It
was an Apostolic head, bald and venerable, and the long silvery hair
flowed on his shoulders and a long white beard fell upon his breast.
His face was handsome and striking, keen yet benevolent, the finely
pencilled eye-brows still dark and a beautiful benevolent loving look
lighted up his fine dark blue eyes when they rested upon you.

He is a very remarkable-looking man, half hermit, half enchanter.

Rev. Francis Kilvert (1874)

Alfred Tennyson Accompanies William Allingham on a Literary Pilgrimage

Friday, August 23 – Very fine. Steamer 11.40 to Yarmouth (Isle of
Wight). Tennyson on the quay, also his brother Frederick and two
daughters. A.T. is going to Lyme Regis alone.

'I have wanted to see the Cobb there ever since I first read *Persuasion*. Will you come?'

Can I possibly? Yes, I will!

We cross to Lymington. I rush up and make hasty arrangements at
Custom-House and lodgings; then off go A.T. and I, second class, to
Dorchester. A.T. smokes. (T. is a great novel reader, very fond of
Scott, but perhaps Miss Austen is his prime favourite.)

In our carriage a cockney Clock-winder, who gets out at every Station to regulate the Railway Company's clock.

Once safely *incognito* T. delights in talking to people, but touch
his personality and he shuts up like an oyster. Shall we stay tonight
at Dorchester? T. vacillates, at last agrees. We go to the 'Antelope'
which produces a pint of good port at dinner. The twilight being fine
I propose that we should visit William Barnes, whom T. personally
knows, and whose poems in the Dorset dialect T. knows and likes. I
show the way to Came Vicarage, where I had enjoyed hospitality from
a Saturday to a Monday a year or two before.

Barnes himself lets us in or comes out at once into the passage - 'Here's an honour!' Little Miss Barnes and Mrs Shaw, a married daughter, appear. B. says, 'put out something! put out something!' with hospitable fervour, tho' we lack no bodily refreshment. Barnes himself, by the way, though not a tee-totaller, is an abstemious man, very plain and inexpensive in his diet. We are pressed to stay but can't. Then we go. Barnes with us to near Dorchester, talking of British Antiquities, Wareham, Sun-worship, etc.

Saturday, August 24 – Dorchester – To Maiden Newton – Bridport. We start off to walk to Lyme Regis, leaving bag to come by carrier. Uphill, view of sea, down to Chidiock, pretty village, old church, flowery houses. We push on (as like two tramps as need be) along the dusty road to Martin's Lake, sea on one hand, shore hills on the other. Down a long hill to Charmouth, where we have beer and cheese in a little inn, then T. smokes in the porch and chats to the waitress. She says she is from the Isle of Wight. 'So am I,' says T., – 'what part?' 'From Cowes,' says the girl. 'I come from Freshwater,' says T., which surprises me, – but he revels in the feeling of anonymosity. We see Lyme below us and take a field-path.

Down into Lyme Regis, narrow old streets, modest little Marine Parade. 'The Cups' receives us in the fair plump good-humoured person of a House-Keeper Barmaid. T. gets a good bedroom and I a tolerable one; we go into garden sloping down-hill and out by some back steps to a Mrs Porter's, where the F. Palgraves are lodging – not in.

Sunday, August 25 – Lyme Regis. Very fine. T. up first and at my door. He has been on the Cobb, and eats a hearty breakfast. We go down to the Cobb, enjoying the sea, the breeze, the coast-view of Portland, etc., and while we sit on the wall I read to him, out of *Persuasion*, the passage where Louisa Musgrove hurts her ankle.

William Allingham (1867)

Wordsworth at Racedown

While we were with [Wordsworth] he relaxed the rigour of his philosophic nerves so much as to go a-Coursing several times, and I assure you did not eat the unfortunate Hares with less relish because he [had] heard them heave their death groans.

Azariah Pinney (in correspondence, 1796)

The Fleur de Lys

Coming late at night into Cranborne Rupert Brooke and his companion failed to find the inn they had chosen from the guide-book because of its name.

In Cranborne town two inns there are,
And one the Fleur-de-Lys is hight[1],
And one, the inn Victoria,
Where, for it was alone in sight,
We turned in tired and tearful plight
Seeking for warmth, and company,
And food, and beds so soft and white -
These things are at the Fleur-de-Lys.

Where is the ointment for the scar?
Slippers? and the table deftly dight?
Sofas? tobacco? soap? and ah!
Hot water for a weary wight?
Where is the food, in toil's despite?
The golden eggs? the toast? the tea?
The maid so pretty and polite?
These things are at the Fleur-de-Lys.

Oh, we have wandered far and far,
We are fordone and wearied quite,
No lamp is lit; there is no star.
Only we know that in the night
We somewhere missed the faces bright,
The lips and eyes we longed to see;
And Love, and Laughter, and Delight,
These things are at the Fleur-de-Lys.

Prince, it is dark to left and right.
Waits there an inn for you and me?
Fine noppy ale and red firelight?
These things are at the Fleur-de-Lys.

Rupert Brooke (1887-1915)

[1] named

10 · RIVERS, VALLEYS AND HARBOURS

In any list of the county treasures of Dorset Poole Harbour must come very near the top. Seen from the heights of Purbeck it is a magnificent spectacle, particularly when sunlight picks out its islands. The largest of them, Brownsea – or Branksea to give it its historical name – has attracted many visitors, and continues to do so. Three hundred years ago Celia Fiennes was mainly interested in the island's copperas industry. Today's visitors are more likely to be drawn to a summertime Shakespearean performance or the birds conserved by the Dorset Wildlife Trust.

The waters of Poole Harbour are not fed by the county's greatest river, the Stour, which at Corfe Mullen swings away eastwards through Wimborne, but by the Piddle and the Frome rivers which converge at Wareham. It is to Frome Vale that Hardy gave the name 'The Valley of the Great Dairies'.

The Stour has many moods. Michael Drayton in his Poly-Olbion celebrated its wandering course through Blackmore Vale, gathering its tributaries, the Lidden and the Divelish near Sturminster Newton, and at Wimborne being joined by the Allen flowing in from Cranborne Chase. Hardy lived for a time beside the Stour at Sturminster and liked to row a boat on it. Llewelyn Powys thought it the friendliest of English rivers, but Peter Beckford saw the violence that comes with a high flood.

Brownsea in 1687

From thence [Poole] by boate we went to a little Isle called Brownsea 3 or 4 leagues off, where there is much Copperice[1] made, the stones being found about the Isle in the shore in great quantetyes, there is only one house there which is the Governours, besides little fisher-mens houses, they being all taken up about the Copperice workes; they gather the stones and place them on the ground raised like the beds of gardens, rows one above the other, and are all shelving so that the raine disolves the stones and it draines down into trenches and pipes made to receive and convey it to the house; that is fitted with iron panns foursquare and of a pretty depth at least 12 yards over, they place iron spikes in the panns full of branches and so as the liquor boyles to a candy it hangs on those branches: I saw some taken up it look't like a vast bunch of grapes, the coullour of the Copperace not being much differing, it lookes cleare like suger-candy, so when the water is boyled to a candy they take it out and replanish the panns with more liquor; I do not remember they added anything to it only the stones of Copperice disolved by the raine into liquour as I mention'd at first; there are great furnaces under, that keeps all the panns boyling; it was a large room or building with severall of these panns; they do add old iron and nailes to the Copperass Stones. This is a noted place for lobsters and crabs and shrimps, there I eate some very good.

Celia Fiennes, 1687

Poole Harbour

The pool or bay is about seven miles long and four broad, the entrance not being above three quarters of a mile broad; opposite to it is Branksey Island, commonly called Brown Island; it is about four miles round, and there is a neglected block house in it; it is the property of Mr Lock of Portsmouth. One Mr Brock took part of it lately, and dug tobacco pipe clay, which is found in many parts about Pool, in the Isle of Purbeck, and near Wareham; he also made tyles of clay in the island,

[1] Copperas is green vitriol, used in dyeing, tanning and making ink. Copperas stone is iron pyrites or marcasite

which abounds in rabbits. Near it is Fuzy Island, about a mile round, and west of that Green Island, half a mile in circumference. Towards the west end is Black Island, a mile round. All the islands are heathy ground, and afford plenty of heath turf.

Richard Pococke (Travels through England, 1754)

A Landing on Brownsea

Eugenia Wynne was staying at Kingston Hall, now Kingston Lacy, when she made an expedition to Brownsea Island, part of the Bankes' substantial estates in Dorset, on 15 October 1803.

This is the day of the spring tides and on which the French are expected to land. We however went a little expedition which the maids of the house thought very venturesome. Mrs Bankes, Mr Butler, the two girls and myself drove to Poole and embarked in the regulating Captain's boat for Brownsea island, which is within Poole Harbour. We had a pleasant sail there and asked leave to land and see the island, a favour which a kind of Savage, Mr Miles (to whom Mr Sturt had let it) perpetually refuses. He allowed us to land but no admittance in the Castle could we get. We were turned from the door by a kind of Dame Leonarda, who is the mother of the woman Mr Miles keeps, and who cooks the dinner which her daughter proudly eats. In vain Mrs Bankes was not sparing of the terms *ungentlemanlike* and *blackguard*, the dragon would not be mollified, and after taking a short turn round the Island we embarked again laughing very heartily at the thought of being turned away.

Eugenia Wynne (Diary 1803)

Modern Brownsea

The largest island in Poole Harbour, which many people still call Branksea, is now part of Studland parish, part of Purbeck again. Its ochre cliffs of gravels, sands and clays topped with the deep greens of trees, already exploited by Lord Mountjoy's copperas or green vitriol and alum-boiling industries, by pipe-clay pits and brick-works, passed from one private owner to another after the Restoration. In my childhood it was haunted by rumours, and protected against all-comers, except Scouts and soldiers, by Mrs Bonham-Christie, the recluse. On her death in 1961 it was feared that a holiday camp might take it over, but her grandson offered it to the Treasury in lieu of death duties. The family pier's Tudor-style watch-towers now welcome visitors and the castellated village on the eastern shore houses the National Trust shop and information office. Seen through an em-battled gatehouse, the castle, rebuilt after a fire of 1896, is the summer preserve of employees of the John Lewis Partnership. Daffodil Field and Peacock Hill both live up to their names; wild and golden pheasants inhabit Beech Valley and Rhododendron Tunnel; and red squirrels chatter in the pine woods where Mad Benson, eminent eighteenth-century lunatic and patron of the arts, is reputed to have practised the black arts. Near Devil's Den Scouts and other youth organisations pitch their tents where Baden-Powell held the first Scout camp in 1907. Shard Point is well named, for it is entirely pebbled with broken pottery and a trackless tramway runs from William Pit, the clayworks and ruined kilns to New Pottery Pier on the west; overgrown bones of workers' cottages stand at Maryland, and near Seymer's Pier and the brickworks on the north shore. Old pyrites mine-shafts fed the copperas works there, but the claims of industry have long since given way to the claims of nature, for the northern half of Brownsea is a reserve run by the Dorset Naturalist Trust. Their headquarters is the Villa between the heronry, the second largest in Britain, and St Andrew's Bay which Colonel Waugh, who invested in clay and built the fussy St Mary's Church before going bankrupt, attempted to reclaim at great expense. Its hundred acres have reverted to marshland inhabited by terns, avocets and curlews, as surely as Humphrey Sturt's eighteenth-century clover fields have been overtaken by bracken. The island is a bizarre mix of dense growth and open space, of nature and nurture, industry and neglect; wildlife is pam-pered, and the signs of man's enterprise grow dimmer every year.

Paul Hyland (Purbeck: The Ingrained Island, 1978)

The Valley of Great Dairies

It was two hours, owing to sundry wrong turnings, ere Tess found herself on a summit commanding the long-sought-for vale, the Valley of Great Dairies, the valley in which milk and butter grew to rankness, and were produced more profusely, if less delicately, than at her home – the verdant plain so well watered by the river Var or Froom.

It was intrinsically different from the Vale of Little Dairies, Blackmoor Vale, which, save during her disastrous sojourn at Tantridge, she had exclusively known till now. The world was drawn to a larger pattern here. The enclosures numbered fifty acres instead of ten, the farmsteads were more extended, the groups of cattle formed tribes hereabout; there only families. These myriads of cows stretching under her eyes from the far east to the far west outnumbered any she had ever seen at one glance before. The green lea was speckled as thickly with them as a canvas by Van Alsloot or Sallaert with burghers. The ripe hue of the red and dun kine absorbed the evening sunlight, which the white-coated animals returned to the eye in rays almost dazzling, even at the distant elevation on which she stood.

The bird's-eye perspective before her was not so luxuriantly beautiful, perhaps, as that other one which she knew so well; yet it was more cheering. It lacked the intensely blue atmosphere of the rival vale, and its heavy soils and scents; the new air was clear, bracing, ethereal. The river itself, which nourished the grass and cows of these renowned dairies, flowed not like the streams in Blackmoor. Those were slow, silent, often turbid; flowing over beds of mud into which the incautious wader might sink and vanish unawares. The Froom waters were clear as the pure River of Life shown to the Evangelist, rapid as the shadow of a cloud, with pebbly shallows that prattled to the sky all day long. There the water-flower was the lily; the crowfoot here.

Thomas Hardy (Tess of the d'Urbervilles, 1891)

The Stour in 1622

Thus thinking, livelie Stour bestirres her tow'rds the maine;
Which lidden leadeth out: then *Dulas* beares her traine
From Blackmore, that at once their watery tribute bring:
When, like some childish wench, she, looselie wantoning,
With tricks and giddie turnes seems to in-ile the shore
Betwixt her fishfull banks, that forward shee doth scour,
Until she lastlie reach clear *Alen* in her race,
Which calmlie commeth down from her dear Mother chace,

Of *Cranburn* that is call'd; who greatly joyes to see
A riveret borne of her for Stour's should reck'ned bee,
Of that renowned flood, a favourite highlie grace't.
Whilst Cranburn for her child so fortunatelie plac't,
With ecchoes everie way applauds her Alen's state,
A sudden noise from *Holt* seems to congratulate
With Cranburn for her brooke so happily bestow'd:
Where to her neighbouring chase, the curteous forrest
    show'd
So just conceived joy, that from each rising hurst,
Where many a goodlie oake had carefullie been nurst,
The sylvans in their songs their mirthfull meetings tell,
And satires, that in slades and gloomy dimbles dwell,
Runne whooting to the hills to clappe their ruder hands.

Michael Drayton (Poly-Olbion, 1622)

'Dulas', Divelish; 'Holt', Holt Forest; 'Hurst', a wood; 'Dimble', shady dell or dingle;
'Slade', valley, dell or dingle; 'Satires'. satyrs.

The Stour at Sturminster Newton

A flooded river after the incessant rains of yesterday. Lumps of froth
float down like swans in front of our house. At the arches of the large
stone bridge the froth has accumulated and lies like hillocks against the
bridge; then the arch chokes, and after a silence coughs out the air and
froth, and gurgles on.

Thomas Hardy (The Life of Thomas Hardy 12 November, 1877)

The Friendly Stour

Bagbere, the little hamlet where William Barnes was born, is situated
on the banks of the River Stour, and his poetry is almost entirely
concerned with the fields, homesteads, straw-strewn bartons and
grassy honeysuckle lanes that are within walking distance of that most
lovely river. Indeed there are many people who find it difficult to
dissociate his poetry from its slowly moving water: waters whose
muddy bottoms have from the earliest days given such good har-
bourage to the coarser kinds of fish; to eels and leather-mouthed chub,

and red-dorsal-finned roach. Of all English rivers, the River Stour is the most friendly. Along under its sweet alder-shaded pools no danger ever lurks; no evil undercurrents ever disturb its wide, cider-coloured reaches, as by wood and "drong," by park and flowering meadow, it winds its way towards the Channel, with no other purpose, it would seem, than to fill with good Stour milk the heavy udders of the dairy cows that frequent the margins of its glimmering levels, where, all day long, over the flat water-lily leaves, dragon-flies, red and blue, hover aslant.

Llewelyn Powys (Thirteen Worthies, 1924)

The Dangerous Stour

The river Stower frequently overflows its banks, and is also very rapid, and very dangerous. The flood, that morning, though sudden, was extensive. The neighbouring meadows were all laid under water, and only the tops of hedges appeared. There were posts to direct us to the bridge, but we had a great length of water to pass before we could get at it; it was, besides, so deep, that our horses almost swam; and the shortest legged horses, and longest legged riders, were worst off. – The hounds dashed in as usual; and were immediately carried, by the rapidity of the current, a long way down the stream. The huntsman was far behind them; and as he could go but slow, he was constrained to see his hounds wear themselves out in a useless contention with the current, in endeavouring to get to him. It was a shocking scene; many of the hounds, when they reached the shore, had entirely lost the use of their limbs; for it froze, and the cold was intolerable. Some lay as if they were dead, and others reeled, as if they had been drinking wine. Our distress was not yet complete; the weakest hounds, or such as were most affected by the cold, we now saw entangled in the tops of the hedges, and heard their lamentations. Well-known tongues! and such as I had never before heard without pleasure. It was shocking to see their distress, and not know how to relieve them. A number of people, by this time, were assembled by the river side, but there was not one amongst them that would venture in. However, a guinea, at last, tempted one man to fetch out a hound that was entangled in a bush, and would otherwise have perished. Two hounds remained upon a hedge all night, yet they got together before the morning; when, the flood abating, they were found closely clasping each other, and without doubt, it was the little heat they could afford each other, that kept both alive. We lost but one hound by this unlucky expedition, but we lost all our terriers. They were seen to sink, their strength not being sufficient to resist the two enemies they had to encounter, powerful, when combined, – the severity of the cold, and the rapidity of the stream.

Peter Beckford (Thoughts on Hunting, 1781)

II · WORTHIES AND UNWORTHIES

To select a dozen candidates is an invidious task. One looks for some touch of originality at least to make a life memorable – and if there were noble endeavour, so much the better. But we also cherish the eccentric and the rascal in the memories we like to keep warm. Who does not relish Lord Shaftesbury's portrait of Henry Hastings?

Pride of place goes to John Hutchins, whose History of Dorset *puts every Dorset writer in his debt. A group of scientists follow, led by an outstanding archaeologist. Hardy in old age is portrayed by T.E. Lawrence, who is himself described by E.M. Forster. There is a literary twilight at Boscombe where two of Shelley's sisters are staying with the poet's son, and an echo from the Civil War recalls the intrepid woman who defended Corfe Castle.*

A Worthy of the First Rank

In the person of the Rev. John Hutchins, M.A., we have a Dorset Worthy of the first rank, inasmuch as he combines in himself literary qualifications and also antiquarian knowledge of the highest distinction; moreover he was born, lived and died in Dorset, having first seen the light at Bradford Peverell, near Dorchester, in 1698, and dying, presumably at Wareham, in 1773. Although he thus lived beyond the allotted span of man, we cannot but marvel at the enormous amount of work which Hutchins has left as a testimony of his industry and his knowledge, in the famous "History of Dorset" – four volumes, folio. This work is so well-known, and it may be added, so voluminous, that it is out of the question to deal with it here. The index of persons mentioned alone numbers some eight thousand names. As was said of Wren, *If you want his monument, look at St. Paul's,* so we may say of Hutchins, *If you want to know what he was, look at his "History of Dorset."*

J.J. Foster (Wessex Worthies, 1920)

General Augustus Pitt-Rivers

In the study of what I may call 'buried history' Pitt-Rivers is the bridge between the old world of science and the new. Personally, he was a benevolent but stern survival from the feudal age. I have known two of his associates, and through them I well understand the unquestioned and unquestioning tyranny with which he ruled. He was right with such a righteousness as only the Victorian era could produce. It is not mere legend that in his presence, his workmen stood to attention at their shovels like his own grenadiers. At the same time behind the martinet was the humble enquiring scholar, confessing, for example, without false shame or concealment the vital post-holes which, in retrospect, he has missed in the uncovering of some ancient homestead, and cataloguing with carefully hoarded experience and ever increasing skill the miserable scraps of ancient humanity which his spade was constantly bringing to light. At their best, so detailed and exact are his records that, more than half a century later, they can be, and have been, broken down and analysed afresh so that, in the light of modern knowledge, new and valuable historical inferences have been drawn from them.

That this rare thing can be done is due to the principle which, as he himself proclaims, underlay his work. He set out to record everything that he found, however insignificant to one working in the year 1890 it may have appeared. Therein lies the genuine humility of the true scholar. He was in fact dealing with remote societies as squalid as those of peripheral ancient Britain could be; the early food-gatherers of Alaska were scarcely more limited in their range of expression.

From such material, information had to be wrung drop by drop by sheer intellectual grasp, by an imagination that found its exercise in an enlarged understanding of the manifestations and processes of ordinary, unheroic human destiny. Pitt-Rivers chose men; Darwin chose pigeons and earthworms; but it is not altogether unfair to say that the assured place occupied by Darwin in the history of natural science is held by Pitt-Rivers in the humanistic science which we call by the clumsy name of archaeology.

Sir Mortimer Wheeler (a radio broadcast in 1953)

Pioneer of Vaccination

Inland from Winspit is the queer, dun hamlet of Worth Matravers, built wholly of stone, but boasting a few trees. The landscape around it is reduced to two elements only – bare grass and the sea. In the burial ground of the beautiful Norman church lies one Benjamin Jesty, who died in 1816, and who was "the first person who introduced the cowpox by inoculation, and who from his great strength of mind made the experiment from the cow on his wife and two sons in the year 1774." The epitaph says nothing of the greater strength of mind shown by his wife and her two sons in submitting themselves to this hazard, nor how it came to pass that the iron-minded Benjamin did not first try the experiment upon himself.

Frederick Treves (Highways and Byways in Dorset, 1906)

Mary Anning

When, in 1810, Richard Anning died, his widow was left with several children to support, Mary, aged ten, being the eldest. We do not hear of Mary attending school after this date; but in the same year, carrying home an ammonite which she had found on the beach, she met a lady, who 'seeing the fossil in her hand, offered her half-a-crown for it, which she accepted, and from that moment fully determined to go down "upon beach" again.' Thus began her independent career as a collector and vendor of fossils, finally to become, in the words of a contemporary writer, 'the most eminent female fossilist.' But she did not rely entirely upon casual visitors for her trade. Local residents or partial residents were already interested in geology, as well as her fellow townsman, De la Beche. Colonel Birch, after whom a

characteristic local ammonite was named, was a frequent visitor, and
we know that he purchased fossils from Mary Anning, as did H.H.
Henley, the Lord of the Manor, whose name was used for one of the
'Green Ammonites.' To collect fossils as a whole-time profession was
something new a hundred years ago; and for a woman to have profes-
sional geological leanings was phenomenal: witness Maria Hack, who,
writing in 1832, says, 'It is certainly uncommon to hear of a lady
engaging in such a fatiguing, hazardous pursuit; and I think few would
be found willing to undertake a personal examination of the cliffs,
especially in the depths of winter'; and Edward Pidgeon, in *The Fossil
Remains of the Animal Kingdom,* writes of the 'arduous and zealous
exertions of this female fossilist in her laborious and sometimes dangerous pursuit.'

We may, then, picture Mary Anning between 1810 and 1811 as-
siduously collecting fossils and selling them locally, but as yet hardly
known outside Lyme itself. In 1811, however, being then but eleven
years old, Mary was fortunate in finding an associated skeleton of the
marine reptile, now known as *Ichthyosaurus.* Hiring men to disengage
it from the stratum in which it lay, she sold it for £23 to Mr Henley,
who in turn gave it to Bullock's Museum at the Egyptian Hall in
Piccadilly.

Thus Mary Anning began to become famous outside her native town;
and we soon hear of her coming into touch with pioneer geologists,
besides De la Beche, who were interested in the fauna of the Lias.

She supplied other palaeontologists, besides those that have been
mentioned, with fossils, vertebrate and invertebrate; and she had a still
more exalted patron. The King of Saxony visited Lyme in 1844, accompanied by his physician, Dr Carus, who has left account of the incident:

> We had alighted from the carriage, and were proceeding along
> on foot, when we fell in with a shop in which the most remark-
> able petrefactions and fossil remains – the head of an Ich-
> thyosaurus, beautiful ammonites, etc., were exhibited in the
> window. We entered, and found a little shop and adjoining
> chamber completely filled with fossil productions of the coast. It
> is a piece of great fortune for the collectors when the heavy
> winter rains loosen and bring down large masses of the projecting
> coast. When such a fall takes place, the most splendid and rarest

fossils are brought to light, and made accessible almost without labour on their part. In the course of the past winter there had been no very favourable slips; the stock of fossils on hand was therefore smaller than usual: still I found in the shop a large slab of blackish clay, in which a perfect Ichthyosaurus of at least six feet was embedded. This specimen would have been a great acquisition for many of the cabinets of Natural History on the Continent, and I consider the price demanded - £15 sterling – as very moderate. I was anxious at all events to write down the address, and the woman who kept the shop, for it was a woman who had devoted herself to this scientific pursuit, with a firm hand wrote her name 'Mary Anning' in my pocket-book, and added, as she returned the book into my hands, 'I am well known through-out the whole of Europe.'

W.D. Lang

Thomas Hardy in Old Age

Peccavi: but always that happens. Look upon me as a habitual incorrigible sinner: and blame upon yourself part of this last silence: for in your letter to me (that which caused the silence) you said 'Tell me about Max Gate' [*Thomas Hardy's house*] – and I can't! The truth seems to be that Max Gate is very difficult to seize upon. I go there as often as I decently can, and hope to go on going there so long as it is within reach: (Sundry prices I've paid in Coy Office for these undefended absences) but description isn't possible. Hardy is so pale, so quiet, so refined into an essence: and camp is such a hurly-burly. When I come back I feel as if I'd woken up from a sleep: not an exciting sleep, but a restful one. There is an unbelievable dignity and ripeness about Hardy: he is waiting so tranquilly for death, without a desire or ambition left in his spirit, as far as I can feel it: and yet he entertains so many illusions, and hopes for the world, things which I, in my disillusioned middle-age, feel to be illusory. They used to call this man a pessimist. While really he is full of fancy expectations.

Then he is so far-away. Napoleon is a real man to him, and the country of Dorsetshire echoes that name everywhere in Hardy's ears. He lives in his period, and thinks of it as the great war: whereas to me that nightmare through the fringe of which I passed has dwarfed all memories of other wars, so that they seem trivial, half-amusing in-cidents. Also he is so assured. I said something a little reflecting on Homer: and he took me up at once, saying that it was not to be despised: that it was very kin to *Marmion* ... saying this not with a grimace, as I would say it, a feeling smart and original and modern, but with the most tolerant kindness in the world. Conceive a man to whom Homer and Scott are companions: who feels easy in such presences.

And the standards of the man! He feels interest in everyone, and veneration for no-one. I've not found in him any bowing-down, moral or material or spiritual.

Yet any little man finds this detachment of Hardy's a vast compli-ment and comfort. He takes me as soberly as he would take John Milton (how sober that name is), considers me as carefully, is as inter-ested in me: for to him every person starts scratch in the life-race, and Hardy has no preferences: and I think no dislikes, except for the people who betray his confidence and publish him to the world.

Perhaps that's partly the secret of that strange house hidden behind its thicket of trees. It's because there are no strangers there. Anyone who does pierce through is accepted by Hardy and Mrs Hardy as one whom they have known always and from whom nothing need be hid.

For the ticket which gained me access to T.H. I'm grateful to you - probably will be grateful always. Max Gate is a place apart: and I feel it all the more poignantly for the contrast of life in this squalid camp. It is strange to pass from the noise and thoughtlessness of sergeants' company into a peace so secure that in it not even Mrs Hardy's tea-cups rattle on the tray: and from a barrack of hollow senseless bustle to the cheerful calm of T.H. thinking aloud about life to two or three of us. If I were in his place I would never wish to die: or even to wish other men dead. The peace which passeth all understanding; – but it can be felt, and is nearly unbearable.

However, here is enough of trying to write about something which is so precious that I grudge writing about it. T.H. is an experience that a man must keep to himself.

I hope your writing goes: that your household goes: that your peace of mind grows. I'm afraid that last does not. Yet I have achieved it in the ranks at the price of stagnancy and beastliness: and I don't know, yet, if it is worth it.

T.E. Lawrence (Letter to Robert Graves, 1923)

T.E. Lawrence at Clouds Hill

T.E. liked to meet people upon a platform of his designing. In my own case it was the platform of aesthetic creation, where I had to figure as a great artist and he was a bungling amateur. This did not suit me in the least, but protests were useless, and after all the important thing was to meet.

We met for the first time in 1921, but then the platform was political. I was having lunch at the Emir Feisal's in Berkeley Square – at him rather than with him, since my virtual host was an old Syrian friend who had gone on his staff. Feisal was absent through most of the meal, owing to business at the Colonial Office. He returned towards the end, and with him came a small fair-haired boy, who seems at this interval of time to have been holding a top-hat. This boy rapped out encouraging words about the Middle East: all would go well now that Winston Churchill was in power. Colonel Lawrence! I wrote a letter afterwards, and said how glad, how proud, I had been to meet him, and had no reply.

In 1924 he lent Siegfried Sassoon a copy of the double column edition of the *Seven Pillars*, and Sassoon asked his permission to send it on to me. He agreed, for he had read a Forster novel, *Howards End*, and it was the real thing, though was not the author long since dead? Better informed in all ways about himself, I was most careful not to praise the *Seven Pillars* when writing to him. I thought it a masterpiece, but to have said so would have been fatal. I restricted myself to detail, and analysed particular sentences and paragraphs, chiefly from the point of view of style. This was well taken, and a suitable platform for our intercourse was thus provided.

As a result of my letter I went down into Dorsetshire and stayed at an inn, of course at his expense. By now he was a private in the Tanks Corps. He turned up while I was having supper, rubicund, clumpier, and rather disconcerting. We must have shaken hands, but he had a bad handshake, and he did not like being touched (by me anyhow); in later years I realized this, and touched him as seldom as possible. Now he spoke: 'It is never very easy to make me eat' was almost his first remark. We were both of us shy. Presently he revealed the existence of Clouds Hill, and I called there the following day. From that moment things went pleasantly. I got on well with my fellow-guests, who were his fellow-soldiers, and felt very happy there. A good early-model gramophone, a nightjar on the roof, fires of rhody-wood, food out of tins eaten as we walked about the upper room, water or tea drunk out of black cups – those are some of my memories. I cannot arrange them, for I was at Clouds Hill several times, once without him. No alcohol, no low talk – and yet at moments T.E. could be bawdy, bringing it in so mischievously and quickly that one could hardly believe one's ears, and was left accusing one's own dirty mind.

The last meeting of all was by the turnstiles of the National Gallery. He was in civvies – a stocky quizzical figure, turning his head slightly until I recognized him. He was out of the service at last and had been hurting his hand against a reporter's face at Clouds Hill. He invited me to stay there again – we hadn't met for a couple of years. We went on to see Epstein's 'Christ' which he remarked would be publicly convenient for birds and then we ate an omelette at a French restaurant in Wardour Street. Our talk was of the impending prosecution of James Hanley's novel, *Boy*. I think that he allowed me to pay for the omelette and that we parted for ever outside another picture gallery, but our last moment together held no more significance than the first moment at Berkeley Square. What was vivid to me was that I liked him as well as ever and should stay with him soon. The date of my visit was fixed but by the time it arrived his life had ended; I have been once to Clouds Hill since then, and was glad to see the improvements he had made – the leather-covered divan, the turfing, the carved doors to the reservoir – but that is the end.

All these are scraps. The real framework, the place which his spirit will never cease to haunt, is Clouds Hill, and the gay motto over its doorway is the one beneath which I see him at rest.

E.M. Forster (1937)

Note: T.E.L. carved OU OPOVRIC on the lintel at Clouds Hill. The Greek is not readily translated; 'no matter for thought', 'no care' are approximate equivalents.

Rev. Mr. Talman, Vicar of Christchurch

Among the many peculiarities of this thoroughly good-natured and universally esteemed incumbent, one may be specified, which, though exceedingly annoying to himself, was somewhat calculated to excite a smile in others; and that, too, on occasions when perfect gravity would have been more decorous and appropriate:- this was the inexpressible horror which he entertained, at every species of contagious disease; and the alarm that he manifested, at any object connected with infection. I have frequently, in company with other boys, attended the interment of those who had fallen victims to fever, small-pox, measles, or similar disorders; attracted, I am sorry to confess, not so much by the sublime and beautiful service used on such occasions, as by a curiosity to observe the wary arrangements made by the cautious vicar, for averting every possible danger of the disorder being communicated to himself. Whenever burials of this nature occurred, it was Mr. Talman's wont, to fortify himself for the dreaded service, both internally and externally; by swallowing a camphor julap, before he went into the church-yard; and proceeding thither with a lump of the same odoriferous drug in his bosom. He would then enjoin the sexton, to place the sentry-box, from which the service was read, at the distance of at least one hundred yards to the windward of the grave; and, with these precautions, would go through the formulary, in such a tone of thunder, as might not only be heard distinctly by the attendants at the funeral, but would surprise even those, who were walking in the street beyond the churchyard.

Richard Warner (Literary Recollections, 1830)

William Allingham Visits the Shelleys at Boscombe

Friday, October 28 – Up at 7 – fog. Drive to Christchurch, the sun breaking through fog. Enter the great Priory Church and look at the Shelley Monument. Call at the gate of Boscombe in passing and leave Lord Houghton's note of introduction with my card. After luncheon I walked out to Boscombe and found Lady Shelley at home – a small lively pleasant woman, who invited us to dinner for to-morrow.

Saturday, October 29 – Boscombe. Sir Percy and Lady Shelley and *two sisters of Percy Bysshe Shelley.* I sat between them at dinner, having taken in Shelley's favourite sister, who name is spelt 'Hellen.' She was lively and chatty, and I looked at and listened to her with great interest. She is tall, very slender, and must have been graceful and handsome in her youth. I saw, or fancied, a likeness to Shelley. She was sumptuous in light purple silk, which became her. She looked about fifty-six, but must be much more. Her sister, who seemed rather younger, was much less lively. Tennyson's name occurring in conversation, Miss Hellen Shelley let it plainly appear that neither he nor any modern poet was of the least interest in her eyes.

'After Shelley, Byron, and Scott, you know,' she said to me, 'one cannot care about other poets.'

Somebody had once read to her a poem of Tennyson's, which she liked, but she could not remember what it was. It seemed doubtful that she had ever heard of Browning.

Sir Percy Florence Shelley is a rather short, fair and fattish man of forty-five. The nose, which is like his mother's, projects when seen in profile, but the front face is roundish and smooth, with small eyes, and a bald forehead over which the pale light-brown hair is partly drawn. His voice is very quiet but in a high key (the only point reminding one of his father), his words few, and whole manner placid, and even apathetic. He likes yachting and private theatricals, cares little or nothing for poetry or literature. He has a thinly-humorous, lounging, self-possessed, quietly contemptuous manner of comment and narration. When I mentioned Tennyson's poetry, Sir Percy said fellows had bored him a good deal with it at one time. He never read any of it of his own accord – saw no sense in it.

William Allingham (1864)

Henry Hastings of Woodlands

Mr Hastings, by his quality, being the son, brother, and uncle to the Earls of Huntingdon, and his way of living, had the first place amongst us. He was peradventure an original in our age, or rather the copy of our nobility in ancient days in hunting and not warlike times; he was low, very strong and very active, of a reddish flaxen hair, his clothes always green cloth, and never all worth when new five pounds. His house was perfectly of the old fashion, in the midst of a large park well stocked with deer, and near the house rabbits to serve his kitchen, many fish-ponds, and great store of wood and timber; a bowling-green in it, long but narrow, full of high ridges, it being never levelled since it was ploughed; they used round sand bowls, and it had a banqueting-house like a stand, a large one built in a tree.

He kept all manner of sport-hounds that ran buck, fox, hare, otter, and badger, and hawks long and short winged; he had all sorts of nets for fishing; he had a walk in the New Forest and the manor of Christ Church. This last supplied him with red deer, sea and river fish; and indeed all his neighbours' grounds and royalties were free to him, who bestowed all his time in such sports, but what he borrowed to caress his neighbours' wives and daughters, there being not a woman in all his walks of the degree of a yeoman's wife or under, and under the age of forty, but it was extremely her fault if he were not intimately acquainted with her. This made him very popular, always speaking kindly to the husband, brother, or father, who was to boot very wel-come to his house whenever he came. There he found beef pudding and small beer in great plenty, a house not so neatly kept as to shame him or his dirty shoes, the great hall strewed with marrow bones, full of hawks' perches, hounds, spaniels, and terriers, the upper sides of the hall hung with the fox-skins of this and the last year's skinning, here and there a polecat intermixed, guns and keepers' and huntsmen's poles in abundance.

The parlour was a large long room, as properly furnished; on a great hearth paved with brick lay some terriers and the choicest hounds and spaniels; seldom but two of the great chairs had litters of young cats in them, which were not to be disturbed, he having always three or four attending him at dinner, and a little white round stick of fourteen inches long lying by his trencher, that he might defend such meat as he had no mind to part with to them. The windows, which were very large, served for places to lay his arrows, crossbows, stonebows, and other such like accoutrements; the corners of the room full of the best chose hunting and hawking poles; an oyster-table at the lower end; which was of constant use twice a day all the year round; for he never failed to eat oysters before dinner and supper through all seasons: the neighbouring town of Poole supplied him with them. The upper part of this room had two small tables and a desk, on the one side of which was a church Bible, on the other the Book of Martyrs; on the tables were hawks' hoods, bells, and such like, two or three old green hats with their crowns thrust in so as to hold ten or a dozen eggs, which were of a pheasant kind of poultry he took much care of and fed himself; tables, dice, cards, and boxes were not wanting. In the hold of the desk were store of tobacco-pipes that had been used.

On one side of this end of the room was the door of a closet, wherein stood the strong beer and the wine, which never came thence but in single glasses, that being the rule of the house exactly observed, for he never exceeded in drink or permitted it. On the other side was a door into an old chapel not used for devotion; the pulpit, as the safest place, was never wanting a cold chine of beef, pasty of venison, gammon of bacon, or great apple-pie, with thick crust extremely baked. His table cost him not much, though it was very good to eat at, his sports supplying all but beef and mutton, except Friday, when he had the best sea-fish as well as other fish he could get, and was the day that his neighbours of best quality most visited him. He never wanted a London pudding, and always sung it in with 'my part lies therein-a'. He drank a glass of wine or two at meals, very often syrup of gillyflower in his sack, and had always a tun glass without feet stood by him holding a pint of small beer, which he often stirred with a great sprig of rosemary. He was well natured, but soon angry, called his servants bastard and cuckoldy knaves, in one of which he often spoke truth to his own knowledge, and sometimes in both, though of the same man. He lived to a hundred, never lost his eyesight, but always writ and read without spectacles, and got to horse without help. Until past fourscore he rode to the death of a stag as well as any.

Anthony Ashley Cooper, First Earl of Shaftesbury (1621-1683)

Sir James Thornhill

This gentleman, the celebrated painter of the Cupola of St. Paul's and of the Halls of Greenwich Hospital, and Blenheim, was born at Melcombe in 1675. He practised originally as a House Painter, but afterwards applied to historical subjects, and with so much success, that he equalled the best painters of his time. In 1719, he was appointed Historical Painter to George the First, and a few months afterwards received the honour of knighthood. He was employed in several extensive works, but the advantages he derived from them was not always equal to his merit, or his labour. The taste of the age was not favourable to genius; the artist being paid in proportion to the space covered, rather than to the value of the painting. Thus, for the dome of St. Paul's, Sir James was paid 40s. per square yard; and for the Hall of Blenheim, 25s. While painting that of St. Paul's, he approached so nearly to the edge of the scaffold, to observe the effect of his work, that he was saved from being dashed to pieces by his servant, who, seeing his danger, instantaneously cast a pot of colour at the figures, which caused him to rush forward for their preservation; and was thus the means of preserving him from destruction. He died at his seat at Thornhill, near Weymouth, in 1734, leaving a son and a daughter; the latter of whom was married to the celebrated Hogarth.

James Dugdale (The New British Traveller, 1819)

Lady Bankes

In 1635, Lord Chief Justice Sir J. Bankes, ancestor of the present owner, bought Corfe Castle. He did not enjoy quiet possession of it long. After eight years, during 1643, when most of the places in Dorset were in possession of the Parliament, Corfe Castle still held out for the king. And who was the commander there – Prince Rupert, the Earl of Carnarvon, Colonel Goring? No. None of these, nor any man at all, but it was Lady Bankes. Sir John Bankes had been called by the king to attend him at York. So my Lady thought she would try what she could do. The Parliamentarians hoped to get into the castle unawares. They gave out that there was to be a stag hunt in Purbeck, really meaning warfare, not sport. They hoped to find the castle gates open, and that the sham hunting party would be able to gallop in and overcome the few men there. But Lady Bankes got to hear of their plan, and kept the gates shut.

Then early one morning another attempt was made. Forty sailors came to the gates and in the Parliament's name demanded that the four little bits of guns, the largest only a three- pounder, which composed the artillery of the castle, should be given up. Now, in the castle there were only Lady Bankes, her maids, and five men. What of that? She had determined to do what she could. She had the gates shut in the sailors' faces. The little guns were at the time dismounted from their carriages. The maids helped to mount one. It was loaded and fired off. The whistle of the three-pound ball over the sailors' heads was unpleasant. This was not the reception which forty men looked for from five men and a few women. The sailors, in short, sheered off.

After a time a bargain was struck. Lady Bankes was to give up the four guns; and, on the other hand, she was to be left at peace in the castle, and to keep the small arms which were in it. This truce did not last long, but she made good use of it in getting men, provisions, and powder into the castle. Very soon it was again attacked. Sir W. Erle, whom we heard of at Dorchester and Weymouth, led more than 200 men against Corfe, and brought several guns. To resist Sir Walter and his party my Lady had eighty men; and her maids too, who must not be forgotten. Some of the enemy had reason to remember them; for an attempt to scale the walls was on one occasion defeated by the female contingent alone. Lady Bankes and her maids pitched stones and shovelfuls of hot ashes on to the enemy, with such good effect that they could make nothing of their escalade that time. For six weeks the siege went on. The church tower was used as a post for musketeers, and the church lead for their bullets. The men being rather slack about scaling the walls, Sir W. Erle inspirited them by a firkin of "hot water," which cost £1.12s. It is, however, recorded that he took none himself, lest he should be courageous against his will. But all would not avail. My lady was stubborn and spirited, and even the hot water did not reconcile the Parliamentarians to the hot ashes coming into their eyes and down their backs. A rumour arose that the Earl of Carnarvon, as above, with some of the king's forces, was coming. Away fled Sir Walter and his 200 men on August 4, 1643, and took boat for Poole, leaving behind them on the shore 100 horses for a prey to the first-comers.... Colonel Lawrence, of Creech Grange, had been the chief man on Lady Bankes' side in the siege. He now, however, wished to change sides, and escaped out of the castle and joined the Parliamentarians. Colonel Lawrence was not the only one in the castle who was false to Lady Bankes. There was Colonel Pitman, an officer of the garrison, who pretending to bring in reinforcements, really let in a large number of Parliament soldiers. Seeing this, Lady Bankes and her garrison had no choice but to surrender. This was on February 27, 1645, after she had held out nearly two years.

H.J. Moule (Old Dorset, 1893)

12 · BIRDS, BEASTS AND FLOWERS

The great geological diversity of its structure gives Dorset a wide range of habitats for wildlife. Despite its relatively small area it has a richer flora and fauna than some much larger counties. Its sea-cliffs are home territory to ravens and puffins, the heath supports sand lizards, smooth snakes and dartford warblers. Its rare breeding species include Montagu's Harriers and it even has its own butterfly, the Lulworth Skipper – though it has not yet found a W. H. Hudson to do it justice. The chalk downland offers a list of wild orchids to the keen-eyed, and Abbotsbury's famous Swannery must be counted a national treasure.

The Swans of Abbotsbury

I saw the remains of what they call the Abbey and a very large barn belonging to it, built of hewn stone; and on a hill to the south is a beautiful chapel of St Catherine. I was then led to the duckoy close to the Fleet, where the swans used to breed as well as wildfowl, and in the pond in the middle I saw some; but they do not encourage their laying here, because they find them in this place more liable to be destroyed by foxes, which have come in and carried them over the wall. Here that body of water call'd the Fleet ends, making a large bay into the land call'd the West Fleet. This swannery belongs to Mrs Horner, the lady of the manor. They compute that there may be now about 500, and they say there are several laws in relation to destroying them, as a fine of five pounds for takeing an egg; and if any one kills a swan, that the swan being hung up the offender must pay a quantity of wheat sufficient to cover the swan. They lay from five to ten eggs; the first year they [the cygnets] are blackish, the second motled, the third black and white, and the fourth become perfectly white, about which time in the fifth year they begin to lay. The young ones frequently dye, particularly in some years, as many last year; and this year they have not one cygnet. The cock has a broader stroak of black down his red bill then the hen. They fight with their wings, and have a sort of spur at the pinion of the wing, with which they deal their blows, if any attack their young; and they have fights with one another, especially about March, when they choose their mate. They lay their eggs in about a fortnight, and sitt on them six weeks. The old couple keep together till about October, when the young ones are able to shift for themselves, and they keep together till about that time if they loose their young. They make a great noise with their wings in flying, and go frequently and sit on the land, but never at night, when they sleep on the water, never dive but in sport; they often take flights; they feed on weeds, putting their heads under the water for them; they often fly about, and sometimes pitch on the sea; and they go down as far as the mouth of the Fleet, and even into Weymouth Harbour. They [the landowners] are very cautious of having them disturbed when they lay or have young, and for that reason put a rail across the beach to hinder any person from riding on it that way. Mrs Horner has a gamekeeper to take care of the swans and the duckoy. In very severe weather a sort of swan comes, call'd a hooper, which are very little less, but have a sharper head more like a snake. 'Tis supposed they come from the north, commonly from three couple to ten, and associate with the swans.

Richard Pococke (Travels through England, 1754)

Ravens and Peregrines

The White Nose ravens seem entirely to disregard all other fowls. Their dark shadows cross and recross the sloping shoulders of the downs, but they are always flying alone, the male and the female, with solitary, mutual love. In February, when they prepare for their first clutch of eggs, they are self-sufficient, and in mid-winter, when they come in over Swyre Head after a morning's scavenging on the Chesil Beach, it is the same. What a massive self-absorption is suggested by the croak of a raven: no wonder to primitive minds this harsh utterance seemed to conceal hidden meanings, dark occult messages, decrees of a dolorous Fate. There is only one pair of ravens nesting now at White Nose. Each autumn they drive their off- spring westward. These unnatural battles usually take place above the under-cliff, towards Ringstead. I was once told by the late Mr Hardy that when he was a boy it was a common thing to see village people bless themselves as these birds flew above the thatched roofs of their cottages far inland, so that seventy or eighty years ago ravens must have been less rare in Dorset than now.

Aloof though the White Nose ravens are there is one bird that breaks in upon their proud isolation. For some obscure reason the heavy, dark flight of these giants of the air is exasperating to peregrine falcons. The war between the ravens and these hawks is as perennial as the traditional contest between pigmies and cranes. A peregrine falcon will pester a raven in its flight for several miles together, soaring high up above it and then with a deadly swoop darting downwards. I have seen them knock feathers out of the raven's body, but never do serious harm, and it is astonishing how the great bird knows when to turn upon its back in mid-air at the very instant when in its downward rush the peregrine is ready to strike.

Llewelyn Powys (Dorset Essays, 1935)

The Pine-Marten

It is a pretty little beast and of a deep chestnut colour, a kind of polecat, lesse than a fox; and the furre is much esteemed: not much inferior to sables. It is the richest furre of our nation. In Cranborn Chase and at Vernditch are some martens still remaining.

John Aubrey (1626-1697)

The Rhododendron Mile

I went back from Hardy's home, down the combe, up to the by-road
and turned right to get back to the Dorchester-Bournemouth main
road. This road just touches the heath about three miles from Dorchester. It runs up through Yellowham Wood and down through a
rhododendron thicket to Troy Town Farm. From thence decent fields
are on either side and the heath appears on the south only as a plantation of larches and a solitary heath knoll. In late May it is worth
turning right off the main road, at the point where it suddenly develops
a wide grass verge, to run along a rough lane through beech trees. This
lane opens into a road which crosses the heath to the Frome meadows.
On either side there is a wide edging of heather, then a mile-long bank
of impenetrable rhododendrons and a background of young pines.
When the rhododendrons are in flower it makes a royal avenue of
purple against the darkness of the evergreens.

I find it almost impossible to describe it without using words which
sound fantastic. Everyone has seen the effect of a gentle snowstorm on
a well-trimmed garden hedge. The snow turns every sharp line into
graceful curves and smooths away all angles. It hides the skeleton of
the hedge to give the impression of a wall, but a wall of clouds. When
the rhododendrons are in their full glory the blossom makes two long
lines of soft snow, except that the snow is purple, mauve, pink and
white. On a June evening this solitary mile of road through the heath is
lovelier than any garden path I have ever seen. So few people know
about it that it has not yet been necessary to stick up notices forbidding
the picking of the flowers. I hope this book will not bring crowds to
ruin the beauty by breaking off great branches which will die in a
couple of days.

The wonder of the place lies partly in its quietness. In the warm
light of evening you get the smell of the pines, the marvel of the blossom, and a chorus of birdsong which is a foretaste of Paradise.

Ralph Wightman (The Wessex Heathland, 1935)

Stag-Beetles

Here [at Bryanston] are found the Scarabei Cervini, rarely met within these parts, and called here Brianston Bucks.

John Hutchins (1774)

An August Midnight

A shaded lamp and a waving blind,
And the beat of a clock from a distant floor:
On this scene enter – winged, horned, and spined –
A longlegs, a moth, and a dumbledore;
While 'mid my page there idly stands
A sleepy fly, that rubs its hands ...

Thus meet we five, in this still place,
At this point of time, at this point in space.
– My guests besmear my new-penned line,
Or bang at the lamp and fall supine.
'God's humblest, they!' I muse. Yet why?
They know Earth-secrets that know not I.

Thomas Hardy (1899)

Sir Joseph Banks Discovers Stone Curlew, May 1767

In returning home this Morn, just at Blanford Horse Course, saw two Remarkable Birds seeming to be of the genus of Cheradrias. Some Shepherds informed me that they came here to breed but are exceeding difficult to shoot. I could make no particular observation but that they were near as large again as grey Plover, had a white spot in each wing and whistled exceedingly shrill, not unlike a man: the shepherds also informed me that they Laid 2 eggs.

Sir Joseph Banks (1767)

A Mermaid

The sea-shore from Portland to this place [Burton Bradstock], is an open beach; but here the cliffs, which are of stone, rise to a great perpendicular height, and abound with various sorts of fossils. June, 1757, a mermaid was thrown up by the sea, between Burton and Swyre, thirteen feet long. The upper part of it had some resemblance to human form, the lower was like that of a fish: the head was partly like that of a man, and partly like that of a hog. Its fins resembled hands: it had forty-eight large teeth in each jaw, not unlike those in the jaw-bone of a man.

John Hutchins (1774)

The Furze Wren (or Dartford Warbler)

To some who have glanced at a little dusty, out-of-shape mummy of a bird, labelled 'Dartford Warbler,' in a museum, or private collection, or under a glass shade, it may seem that I speak too warmly of the pleasure which the sight of the small furze-lover can give us. He is of the type of the white-throat, but idealized; the familiar brown, excitable Sylvia, pretty as he is and welcome to our hedges in April, is in appearance but a rough study for the smaller, more delicately-fashioned and richly-coloured Melizophilus, or furze-lover. On account of his excessive rarity he can now been seen at his best only by those who are able to spend many days in searching and in watching, who have the patience to sit motionless by the hour; and at length the little hideling, tired of concealment or overcome by curiosity, shows himself and comes nearer and nearer, until the ruby red of the small gem-like eye may be seen without aid to the vision. A sprite-like bird in his slender exquisite shape and his beautiful fits of excitement; fantastic in his motions as he flits and flies from spray to spray, now hovering motionless in the air like the wooing goldcrest, anon dropping on a perch, to sit jerking his long tail, his crest raised, his throat swollen, chiding when he sings and singing when he chides, like a refined and lesser sedge warbler in a frenzy, his slate-black and chestnut-red plumage showing rich and dark against the pure luminous yellow of the massed furze blossoms. It is a sight of fairy-like bird life and of flower which cannot soon be forgotten.

W.H. Hudson (Birds & Man, 1915)

Flowers A-Field

In hay-fields where the hedge-boughs cope
The sunny hedge-bank's flow'ry slope,
out where the prickly wildrose blows,
Above the bloomy bramble-bows,
Some maiden cries, 'The briars prick
My fingers to the very quick;
Come pull me down a wild rose, do,
For I can't cope with it like you!'

And out in meadows, where the hay,
Now nearly dry, is rustling gray,
Before the touch of rake or prongs,
And under women's merry songs;
Then there, as I by chance come by
The laughing girls, I hear them cry,
'Come pull me down a woodbine, do,
For I can't reach it there. Can you?'

And down beside the river's brim,
Where whirling waters softly swim -
Where we can see the bulrush nod
Its club upon its slender rod;
Then there, as merry girls behold
The water-lily's flow'r of gold,
They cry, 'Oh! rake me out one, do,
For I can't reach it in. Can you?'

William Barnes

13 · THE WORK-FOLK

If the rural labourer made an appearance in a novel or a play it was a long-standing tradition that he would be seen as a dimwit, a stunpoll, a be-smocked figure of fun called Hodge. Hardy challenged this stereotype, and out of the earlier shadows have come individual portraits of shepherds and dairymaids and the many independent craftsmen and women who shared the village-life of the farm workers. The Dorset Scene would be woefully incomplete without them.

The Apple Harvest

It was about the middle of the early apple-harvest, and the laden trees were shaken at intervals by the gatherers; the soft pattering of the falling crop upon the grassy ground being diversified by the loud rattle of vagrant ones upon a rail, hen-coop, basket, or lean-to roof, or upon the rounded and stooping backs of the collectors – mostly children, who would have cried bitterly at receiving such a smart blow from any other quarter, but smilingly assumed it to be fun in apples.

Under the trees now stood a cider-mill and press, and upon the spot sheltered by the boughs were gathered Mr Springrove himself, his men, the parish clerk, two or three other men, grinders and supernumeries, a woman with an infant in her arms, a flock of pigeons, and some little boys with straws in their mouths, endeavouring, whenever the men's backs were turned, to get a sip of the sweet juice from the vat.

Thomas Hardy (Desperate Remedies, 1871)

Rural Crafts

In their little cottage homes at Swyre, Burton Bradstock, Puncknowle, Loders, Bradpole, Hamworthy, and elsewhere to the west of the county, we shall find women of all ages making every conceivable type of net, from trammels for the fishing fleets to tennis, football, and hockey nets for sports clubs; from camouflage nets to billiard pockets; from "life-savers" to hammocks.

In these cottages we shall see old women of perhaps eighty or more working side by side with their grand-children, or even, on occasion, their great-grand-children, carrying out a work which they themselves had learnt in early childhood from their parents and grandparents. These "braiders" are following a tradition that is older than Domesday, and, just as Honiton is the "capital" of the Devon lace-makers, so has Bridport been their administrative centre since time immemorial. Indeed, it was on account of her part in providing nets and cables for the Navy that King John granted Bridport her charter in the first place.

It is fascinating to watch these women plying this age-old industry. Here we may see them at work within the snugness of their kitchen living- rooms on a cold winter's day; there we shall find them working from their cottage doors in the warmth of the summer sun. There again, when the net to be made is a particularly large one, we may stumble upon a whole group of them working their way down a street or lane with a single net stretching from porch to porch. The craft is not only confined to the women, though. Sometimes we may meet with an old man, who has toiled perhaps sixty summers or more in the fields, lovingly endeavouring to help his "missus", and so increase their earnings.

One old "braider", who said that she had learnt the work from her mother at the age of eight, told me that every week representatives from the Bridport firms call on these cottagers with supplies of fresh materials and to collect the finished articles, which are then taken back, tarred, and packed for delivery all over the world, an important market being the Newfoundland fisheries.

"Do you make *all* kinds of nets?" I asked.

"Oh, no, sir, not *all*. Some o' we make one sort, and others another."

between you you manage to serve the entire market? Can you
~ much money at this business?"

"Well, sir, us don't do too badly on the whole. Us usually reckons to
make about a shilling an hour."

A shilling an hour, and that for skilled labour! I asked her whether
she would not find it more profitable to change her occupation.

"No, sir, thank'ee. Anyone can scrub a floor, but not everyone can
make a net." She laughed.

Such is the pride of these Dorset folk. You will find men and women
of this kind all over the county: "broom squires" making besoms in
Cranborne Chase; potters at Verwood, who puddle their clay with
their feet as in Tudor times; rush-workers who gather their materials
from the banks of the River Stour for making into dog baskets, church
kneelers, and the like; flax-workers round Shaftesbury; millers who
still process their corn by the power of water wheels.

Norman Wymer (A Breath of England, 1948)

The Handyman

Wanted – A Man-Servant that understands and loves to work in a
Garden, which will be his principal Business. He must be handy, able
to lay a Cloth, and wait at Table, and understand Brewing. N.B. –
have had the Small-Pox, be perfectly sober, well recommended, and
able to write and cast Accounts.

The Western Flying Post, or Sherborne and Yeovil Mercury (1760)

The Hiring Fair

The hiring-fair of recent years presents an appearance unlike that of
former times. A glance up the high street of the town on a Candlemas-
fair day twenty or thirty years ago revealed a crowd whose general
colour was whity-brown flecked with white. Black was almost absent,
the few farmers who wore that shade hardly discernible. Now the
crowd is as dark as a London crowd. This change is owing to the rage
for cloth clothes which possesses the labourers of today. Formerly they
came in smock-frocks and gaiters, the shepherds with their crooks, the
carters with a zone of whipcord round their hats, thatchers with a
straw tucked into the brim, and so on. Now, with the exception of the

crook in the hands of an occasional old shepherd, there is no mark of speciality in the groups, who might be tailors or undertakers' men, for what they exhibit externally.

Having 'agreed for a place', as it is called, either at the fair, or (occasionally) by private intelligence, or (with growing frequency) by advertisement in the penny local papers, the terms are usually reduced to writing: though formerly a written agreement was unknown, and is now, as a rule, avoided by the farmer if the labourer does not insist upon one. It is signed by both, and a shilling is passed to bind the bargain. The business is then settled, and the man returns to his place of work, to do no more in the matter till Lady Day, Old Style – April 6.

Of all the days in the year, people who love the rural poor of the south-west should pray for a fine day then. Dwellers near the highways of the county are reminded of the anniversary surely enough. They are conscious of a disturbance of their night's rest by noises beginning in the small hours of darkness, and intermittently continuing till daylight - noises as certain to recur on that particular night of the month as the voice of the cuckoo on the third or fourth week of the same. The day of fulfilment has come, and the labourers are on the point of being fetched from the old farm by the carters of the new. For it is always by the waggon and horses of the farmer who requires his services that the hired man is conveyed to his destination; and that this may be accomplished within the day is the reason that the noises begin so soon after midnight. Suppose the distance to be an ordinary one of a dozen or fifteen miles. The carter at the prospective place rises 'when Charles's Wain is over the new chimney', harnesses his team of three horses by lantern light, and proceeds to the present home of his coming comrade. It is the passing of these empty waggons in all directions that is heard breaking the stillness of the hours before dawn. The aim is usually to be at the door of the removing household by six o'clock, when the loading of goods at once begins; and at nine or ten the start to the new home is made.

The goods are built up on the waggon to a well-nigh unvarying pattern, which is probably as peculiar to the country labourer as the hexagon to the bee. The dresser, with its finger-marks and domestic evidences thick upon it, stands importantly in front, over the backs of the shaft horses, in its erect and natural position, like some Ark of the Covenant, which must not be handled slightingly or overturned. The hive of bees is slung up to the axle of the waggon, and alongside it the cooking pot or crock, within which are stowed the roots of garden flowers. Barrels are largely used for crockery, and budding gooseberry bushes are suspended by the roots; while on the top of the furniture a circular nest is made of the bed and bedding for the matron and children, who sit there through the journey. If there is no infant in arms, the woman holds the head of the clock, which at any exceptional lurch of the waggon strikes one, in thin tones. The other object of solicitude is the looking-glass, usually held in the lap of the eldest girl. It is emphatically spoken of as the looking-glass, there being but one in the house, except possibly a small shaving-glass for the husband.

The day of removal, if fine, wears an aspect of jollity, and the whole proceeding is a blithe one. A bundle of provisions for the journey is usually hung up at the side of the vehicle, together with a three-pint stone jar of extra strong ale; for it is as impossible to move house without beer as without horses. Roadside inns, too, are patronized, where, during the halt, a mug is seen ascending and descending through the air to and from the feminine portion of the household at the top of the waggon. The drinking at these times is, however, moderate, the beer supplied to travelling labourers being of a preternaturally small brew.

Ten or a dozen of these families, with their goods, may be seen halting simultaneously at an out-of-the-way inn, and it is not possible to walk a mile on any of the high roads this day without meeting several. This annual migration from farm to farm is much in excess of what it was formerly. For example, on a particular farm where, a generation ago, not more than one cottage on an average changed occupants yearly, and where the majority remained all their lifetime, the whole number of tenants were changed at Lady Day just past, and this though nearly all of them had been new arrivals on the previous Lady Day. Dorset labourers now look upon an annual removal as the most natural thing in the world, and it becomes with the younger families a pleasant excitement.

Thomas Hardy (The Dorsetshire Labourer, 1883)

14 · CRANBORNE CHASE AND BLACKMORE VALE

The north east of the county brings together two of its most distinctive landscapes. Cranborne Chase, extending from Salisbury to Blandford, preserves much of its historic character as a game-reserve with a scattered village population and some palatial manor-houses in parkland and well- wooded downs.

Shaftesbury on its ridge is the link connecting the Chase to the very different scene of the Vale of Blackmore. Here the heavy soil and moist atmosphere of the upper reaches of the Stour provide the traditional setting for dairyfarming and – until recently – cider orchards. Treves caught its essence neatly in a phrase – 'the smell of cows is the incense of north Dorset'.

According to H.J. Massingham the road through Cranborne Chase from Salisbury to Blandford offered so much on either side to explore that it required at least a month to complete the journey. Aubrey recalls memories of Sir Philip Sidney riding there when he was at Wilton. A visit to Chettle House, which is open to the public, is a reminder that this was the home of the celebrated sporting parson, William Chafin, whose Anecdotes of Cranborne Chase recapture a bygone age. When Sir Walter Scott visited his friend William Stewart Rose at Mudeford he was so amused by stories of the legendary Mr. Chafin that he wrote a wildly exaggerated but most entertaining satire on this 'parson mad upon sport'.

Among many fine houses Cranborne Manor is perhaps the most

*admired – and certainly most loved by the author Lord David Cecil
who spent his boy-hood there. What once may have surpassed it for
sheer size and opulence was Eastbury House at Tarrant Gunville: most
of Vanburgh's creation was being demolished in 1782 when John Byng
rode past it.*

Cranborne Chase

The great way to see Cranborne Chase and to be imaginatively fired by
the palimpsest of its cultural continuity is to take the high road from
Salisbury to Blandford Forum. A great many people do, but they get
from the one place to the other in less than an hour. You want at least a
month for the journey, so constantly will you be diverted off to the
right hand and the left as you go. Would that I could linger over this
enchanted ground for a hundred pages! Meet first the area of bare
down, once congested with humanity, on the left of the road and immediately south of the great yew forest below Odstock. Six long-lived
cultures have fixed their signatures to it. The first, that of the long
barrows, is richly represented. There are four long barrows here, the
Giant's Grave on Breamore Down, the curious Duck's Nest in the
middle of nowhere north of Rockbourne with its priest-like yew rising
from the undergrowth that covers the mound, and Knap Barrow and
Grans Barrow on the edge of Toyd Down, a mile above the Allen
River. A complete circle of hills surrounds them from Pentridge to
Whitsbury, while their track runs on past the Duck's Nest to Rockbourne Down, where on a clear day you see from Inkpen Beacon to the
gap of Corfe Castle. The country is very wild about them, patched
with scrub, and the three long barrows in sight of each other have a
certain oddity in structure which communicates a strangeness to the
setting. It seems to be the land of the *living* dead.

How many long barrows are there in Cranborne Chase – twenty,
thirty? They top the crests all along our road, staring into space, the
sphinxes of old England – Wor Barrow near Sixpenny Handley, ex-
cavated by Pitt-Rivers, the noble pair on Gussage Cow Down, by the
Bokerly Dyke, on Thickthorn and, the grandest of them all, the Titan
of Pimperne, shaped to a downlike grace. Round barrows are scattered like stars in the sky and of their age are the squareish pastoral

enclosures of Martin Down and the 'Soldier's Ring' in a slight hollow below the edge from which I looked down on the wastes of the New Forest, darker than their wont with rain. The next age follows a thousand years after, but here only a mile away, and witnesses the huge fortifications of Castle Ditches above Whitsbury, clouded with trees. Ackling Dyke speaks the Roman name, the village on Damerham Knoll its subject-people, Bokerly Dyke, an England stripped of its foreign guard and desperately waiting the Saxon terror, while the maze on Mizmaze Down by Breamore carves out in turf the sinuosities of evil a thirteenth-century pilgrim must find his way through to the central hump of Paradise.

The next stop is at the Bokerly Dyke and the main road slices through it. Pitt-Rivers proved that the great ramp was raised and the steep ditch was dug after Rome had shrunk and ebbed from our downs. The defences face north to save all this desirable land from the advance of the West Saxons stationed by the Avon, and it stopped the march of ruin for thirty years.

Oakley Down succeeds and here is spectacle indeed. Beside the road lies the necropolis of an older and longer civilisation than the Celtic or Romano-Celtic. The rough down, overhung by the shoulder of Pentridge, is constellated with barrows – Wor Barrow, huge bell-barrows, the more ordinary bowl barrow and some remarkably fine specimens of disc barrows. Through the formal bank of one of them slices the Roman road on its inflexible way from Old Sarum to Badbury Rings and Dorchester. The causeway or 'agger' with its side ditches remains very distinct along this portion of the Ackling Dyke, a telling illustration of the Roman bondage to rule where the hard chalk made it unnecessary. The Romans were brilliant but pedantic engineers.

Gussage Cow Down lies over the next ridge and still the land belongs to pre-history, for the villages of the Gussages and Tarrants hereabouts are all poked away in narrow defiles and unsuspected pockets of the downs. Witchampton is the best of them in this area, being generously endowed with such antiquities as an abbey barn, a mill and fine old stone bridge, a lych-gate and one of those manor-houses in which Dorset is exceptionally rich. The valley villages of the Dorset downland show the familiar combinations of flint, chalk and brick with clusters of thatched roofs, but the architectural workmanship is inferior to that of Wiltshire, where brick, flint, chalk, pudding stone and sarsens are built in together with bold experiment and resource. Where Dorset excels is in the sounds, honeyed or sonorous, of her village names.

But on Gussage Cow Down is the tracing not of a village but of a town like Woodcuts. All the ages of man in society, but beyond the reach of history, are written on the scarred face of the Down – a Roman halting station, the Celtic town, four round barrows and a disc barrow, a pair of uprearing long barrows that take the whole ridge into their keeping and, best of all, a great Cursus, unique in Dorset. All the dark face of Cranborne Chase, embossed with its hillbrows and of light relieving greens where the bare chalk is supreme, lies open from it to the west and north, while shaggy Pentridge, the Esau of these hills, looks closely down upon it. It is towards Pentridge that the Cursus flows for nearly four miles, two parallel banks and ditches about a hundred yards apart, and the triple and quadruple embankments of the forsaken city cut clean through it, thus revealing the former's earlier tenure of the hill.

If you continue along the main road to Blandford and take the next turning to the left, you meet the Wimborne-Cranborne road at the Horton Inn. Its landlord, standing in front of a ribald and Reformation print of monkish scandals on his wall, once told me that his ancestors were sun-worshippers. What he was referring to were the Knowlton Circles, a little nearer Cranborne. Only one of the four circular earthworks has escaped the plough. In the centre of its perfect round of high ramp and inner ditch stands a deserted little flint church of the early fourteenth century, standing like the moon when, foreboding rain, it is encircled by a wide aura. It is a beautiful example of the continuity of sacred sites, for, with the exception of Oakley Down, Knowlton, with its round barrows, is the only other *locus consecratus* visible on Cranborne Chase. In structure and plan it is a little Avebury without the stones, and, likely enough, timber uprights were set up along the lip of the ditch as substitutes for monoliths of stone. It also reminds you of a magnified disc barrow without the central hump. But who knows what mound or burial chamber was supplanted by the forlorn little church, whose ragged and dismantled walls now admit not worshippers but only the wind and the rain.

H.J. Massingham (*The English Downland, 1936*)

Sir Philip Sidney in Cranborne Chase

In this tract is ye Earle of Pembroke's noble seat at Wilton; but the Arcadia and the Daphne is about Vernditch and Wilton; and these romancy plaines and boscages did no doubt conduce to the hightening of Sir Philip Sydney's phansie. He lived much in these parts, and his most masterly touches of his pastoralls he wrote here upon the spott, where they were conceived. 'Twas about these purlieus that the muses were wont to appeare to Sir Philip Sydney, and where he wrote down their dictates in his table book, though on horseback. For those nimble fugitives, except they be presently registred, fly away, and perhaps can never be caught again. But they were never so kind to appeare to me, though I am the usufructuary: [Aubrey held the manor farm of Broad Chalke under a lease from the Earl of Pembroke] it seemes they reserve that grace only for the proprietors, to whom they have continued a constant kindnesse for a succession of generations of the no lesse ingenious than honorable family of the Herberts.

These were the places where our Kings and Queens used to divert themselves in the hunting season. Cranborne Chase, which reaches from Harnham Bridge, at Salisbury, near to Blandford, was belonging to Roger Mortimer, Earle of March: his seate was at his castle at Cranbourne.

John Aubrey (1626-1697)

A Parson Mad Upon Sport

In a copy of William Chafin's Anecdotes of Cranborne Chase *Sir Walter Scott wrote the following –*

Mr Chaffin Author of this admirable Specimen of the Rigmarolical stile of Composition was the son of a parson and in process of time became a parson himself. His first commencement as a sportsman was rather inauspicious – he shot an old woman. He left his game where it dropt without staying to bag it. But when the servant announced as a piece of news that Goody – was shot there was a confession in the boy's looks which made his father exclaim 'There sits the rascal who killed her'. What the Coroner's inquest said is unknown but the father in virtue of his *patris potestas* confined the youth for a month to a garret and bread and water. During this penance he spared some of his bread to bait traps for sparrows and thus solaced the hours of his imprisonment.

As he grew up his passion for hunting increased. In the words of Sir Archie MacSarcann he hunted everything from the flea in the blanket to the elephant in the forest. But his chief sport was afforded by foxes, hares, rabbits and owls. In the two first sports he was only distinguished by superior zeal and science but the other two modes of chase were peculiar. For rabbits he had a little pack of small beagles not exceeding twelve or fourteen inches which he carried to the field in panniers on the horse he himself rode. It often took this lilliputian pack half an hour to kill a rabbit. In the owl-hunting his parishioners acted as the pack. The owl being unkennel'd in a sun-shiny day was pursued by the whole parish in full cry till distressed by the clamour and the glare of light he took shelter in some bush or tree where if it had not been marked down it was soon discovered by the small birds who always dog its flight. Mr Chaffin used to oration his pack on these occasions with the emphatic memento 'No deaths No strong Beer.'

More of this venerable and eccentric son of Nimrod my informer knows not save that he always wore old boots and greasy leathern breeches and in such attire dined with the present King, then Prince of Wales, whose attention he had attracted by rating his Royal Highness in language much more emphatic than courtly for crying the hue of a fox which had broken cover.

> And all these particulars are true I suppose
> Because my informer is Will Stuart Rose
> Who had in his younger days much fun and laughing
> At the whims and the huntings of old Parson Chaffin.
>
> Sir Walter Scott (c.1818)

Cranborne Manor

For me, Cranborne Manor is the first of Dorset country houses. No doubt I am biased in its favour because I was so happy there during the 'long blessed eventless days' of childhood. But I was happy in other places which no longer appeal to me, whereas Cranborne's charm is to me as powerful as ever, though seen now in the unillusioned light of old age. One catches sight of it first as a huddle of grey battlements and russet chimneys, lying in a little patch of leafy rural England, set in a hollow of downland. It is a manor house on the edge of a village, with one of its garden walls opening into the churchyard, and the others – it is surrounded by gardens – standing in the midst of ordinary fields. You turn in out of the village street; and then, two or three hundred yards beyond the gate, on the right-hand side you get your first full view of it. An arch joining two brick Jacobean gatehouses with pointed roofs, opens into a paved flower-scented courtyard at the end of which the front stands up, tall, towered and silver-grey with a little three-arched porch in the middle, carved with a figure of Justice and her scales.

The house is of many dates. The weather-stained turret embedded in the wall west of the porch is a relic of the middle ages, when it was one of the king's hunting lodges. So is the ecclesiastical-looking lancet window on the eastern wall – perhaps a window of the king's private chapel. But Cranborne Manor, as it now presents itself to the world, is the creation of Robert Cecil, first Earl of Salisbury, chief minister of Queen Elizabeth I from whom he bought the house and also of her successor James I in whose reign he began transforming it.

Robert Cecil was one of the most remarkable personalities of his age. A small hunch-back with a pale face and gentle manner, he cut a modest figure besides such magnificent rivals as Essex and Raleigh. But, subtle, purposeful, formidable, he managed to defeat them all: up till his death he maintained his position as the most powerful man in England. Surprisingly he had time left over for his chief hobby, building. He built himself a great palace in London and another at Hatfield. Cranborne was only a sideline, but it was an inspired sideline. The inspiration is apparent both in the south front with its courtyard and gatehouses and even more in the north front. Here the high mediaeval walls are as it were embroidered all over with flights of Jacobean fantasy, showing mainly in the carved buttresses and round the big sculptured loggia surmounted by a coat of arms. All is unsymmetrical and irregular. But the effect is romantically enchanted; and all the more because it overlooks a balustraded terrace with steps leading down to a walled 17th century garden with a pillared gateway at the end of it, opening on a wide view of the countryside. The whole effect is an expression of the lyrical fanciful strain in the imagination of the period, for me the architectural equivalent of Campion's songs or Shakespeare's comedies.

Lord David Cecil (Some Dorset Country Houses, 1985)

A Last View of Vanbrugh's Eastbury House

In my way I passed through the villages of Pimpern, and Tarrant; near which was the magnificent park and seat [Eastbury] of the late Ld Mellcombe, now belonging to Mr Earle [Earl Temple], who has dismantled the park, and is pulling down the great edifice. Near it is a seemingly good hunting seat [Chettle] of Mr Chaffin's, which must be well placed for fox, or hare hunting.

Hon. John Byng (1782)

The Hurdle Makers of Sixpenny Handley

I can remember when there used to be thirty or forty hurdle makers around Handley, and now there's only about fourteen. I've learned five of them – all good hurdle-makers they've turned out, and two of them I'd back against any in the country. But there isn't the demand for hurdles like there used to be.

Dorset used to be a sheep county, and The Chase was famous for its hurdles. But there's no living for a man nowadays in sheep-hurdles. We've had to change our ways and turn to other things. We go in more for fence-work, garden-hurdles. That's a different size of hurdle and we send a lot of them to London. They make very good fences, you know. They'll last eight or ten years – and more than that if you creosote them. And I'll say this – it would take you longer to pull a Chase hurdle apart than it takes us to make them. They're woven together as tight as a basket. That's the art of it – and getting good wood, of course. The woods are put up for auction once a year, in the autumn, and we do buy the timber by the lug. Ten strides wide and ten strides long is four lugs – what we call lugs. And we bid so much a lug. We look round the hazel copses first, to see if we can get the best pieces. We bid for 'em, and sometimes we get 'em, and sometimes we get the rough. Depends on the price. You want about three or four acres for a year's work.

When the auction's over you pay five shillings in the pound for what you've bought and the rest before the next auction. The old rule was to have all your wood cut by the end of March and all out of the woods by June - but now we work in the woods all the year round.

'Buffer' Lucas (in a radio broadcast in 1946)

Blandford Forum

Blandford, our next stage, lies about sixteen miles from Dorchester; and, though not a place of such renowned antiquity, is perhaps a still more agreeable town. It lies within a curve of the river Stour, and is pleasantly seated among meadows and woods. If a person wished to retire from business, where he might have the convenience and pleasures of the town and country united, his choice might waver between Barnstaple, Dorchester and Blandford. If he wished to be near the sea, he will find a pleasant sea-coast at Barnstaple. If airy downs and open country pleased him he might fix at Dorchester. But if he loved meadows and woodlands he must make choice of Blandford.

William Gilpin (Observations on the Western Parts of England, 1798)

From Wimborne to Shaftesbury

The greater part of the road to Blandford is over naked downs, steep chalky hills succeeding to valleys all the way. The country on both sides is most fatiguing to the eye of every one but a fox-hunter. Iris foetidissima is abundant by the road side. The road from Blandford to Shaftesbury is through a fine country, but is extremely hilly.

Bryanston House, J. Portman, Esq – The house, like that of Langton [Langton Long, near Blandford: the seat of 'Squire' J. J. Farquharson] is in a bottom, with the meadows of the Stour and a fine reach of the river in front; but is placed much higher, backed by steeper hills, and commands much bolder ground on the opposite side of the river.

This place is at all times open to all the decently dressed inhabitants of Blandford, and to all other respectable persons. The grassy terraces, called the cliff walks, are scenes of extraordinary dignity and beauty. Besides the views of the river, the park, the country beyond the bridge, and the town of Blandford, they display in the foreground some fine specimens of exotic trees, and of yews, boxes and hollies; the surface of the ground was in some places covered with vigorous plants of scolopendrium, and in others with beds of native violets and prim-roses. In spring the whole of the native woods of this place must afford a rich treat to the botanist.

John Claudius Loudon (In Search of English Gardens, 1833)

It's the Thought that Counts

A loyal address from the town of Shaftesbury to George I concluded with the following words:
'...and Pardon us for Imploring the Almighty that he may *very late* translate you, Our Inestimable Blessing, from this to an Eternal Crown above.'

State Papers of George I (1660-1727)

Shaftesbury: overlooking the Vale of Blackmore

On the southern edge of the ridge is a delightful wooded walk, called Park Walk, from which extends a view surpassed by few in England. This meditative avenue is on the very edge of the height, and it is said to have been a walk in the Abbey Park. At the foot of the hill, below the terrace, lie the thatched roofs of the suburb of St James, with its ample gardens and its quite impressive church. The little settlement suggests a village on a beach as seen from the brink of an over-tower-ing cliff.

The view from the Abbey terrace is across a vast, verdant, undulat-ing valley of the richest pasture land – a plain without a level stretch in it. It ever rolls away into shallow valley and low hill, and now and then a wooded height or the glittering track of a stream. The land is broken up into a thousand fields, fringed by luxuriant hedges. In every hedge are many trees; trees follow every buff-coloured road, and gather around every hamlet or cluster of farm buildings. It is a country of dairies. Everywhere are there cows, for the smell of cows is the incense of North Dorset.

Sir Frederick Treves (1906)

White Hart Silver (1)

From Mapowder the Brooke passeth through deepe and dirtie soyle under King's Stagge Bridge which gott that name upon this occasion: King Henry the Third haveing disported himselfe in the Forrest of Blackmore hee spared one beautifull and goodlie White Harte, which afterwards [John] de la Linde, a neighbour gentleman of antient descent and especiall note, with his companions persueing killed at this place; but hee soone founde howe dangerous it waas to bee twitching a Lion by the eares, for the Kinge tooke soe great indignation against him that hee not onlie punished them with imprisonment and a grevous fine of money, but for this fact hee taxed their lands, the owners of which ever sithence, yearlie untill this daye, paye a rounde summe of money, by way of amerciment unto the Exchequer, called White Harte Silver, in memorie of which this county needeth no better remembrance than the annual payment.

Coker's Survey of Dorsetshire (by Thomas Gerard, died 1634)

White Hart Silver (2)

White hart silver is paid to this day into the Exchequer; myself hath paid a share for the sauce who never tasted any of the meat; so that it seems King's Venison is sooner eaten than digested.

Thomas Fuller (History of the Worthies of England 1608-1661)

The Springs of Blackmore Vale

The land drops four hundred feet very steeply to the Vale of Blackmore. Immediately at the foot of this very steep chalk slope there is a narrow band of greensand soil, often not more than a few hundred yards wide and never more than three miles. It is full of springs, lovely clear water bubbling out of the base of the hill, inexhaustible and never varying more than a degree or two from a temperature of 54°F. In winter it feels warm, and the mist rises from it on a frosty night, while in summer it is so cold that a glass dipped in it is immediately covered with dew. These deep springs of the greensand water all the wide clay vale.

Ralph Wightman (in a radio broadcast in 1944)

The Vale of Blackmoor

This fertile and sheltered tract of country, in which the fields are never brown and the springs never dry, is bounded on the south by the bold chalk ridge that embraces the prominences of Hambledon Hill, Bulbarrow, Nettlecombe Tout, Dogbury, High Stoy, and Bubb Down. The traveller from the coast, who, after plodding northward for a score of miles over calcareous downs and corn-lands, suddenly reaches the verge of one of these escarpments, is surprised and delighted to behold, extended like a map beneath him, a country differing absolutely from that which he has passed through. Behind him the hills are open, the sun blazes down upon fields so large as to give an unenclosed character to the landscape, the lanes are white, the hedges low and plashed, the atmosphere colourless. Here, in the valley, the world seems to be constructed upon a smaller and more delicate scale; the fields are mere paddocks, so reduced that from this height their hedgerows appear a network of dark green threads overspreading the paler green of the grass. The atmosphere beneath is languorous, and is so tinged with azure that what artists call the middle distance partakes also of that hue, while the horizon beyond is of the deepest ultramarine. Arable lands are few and limited; with but slight exceptions the prospect is a broad rich mass of grass and trees, mantling minor hills and dales within the major. Such is the Vale of Blackmoor.

Thomas Hardy (Tess of the d'Urbervilles, 1891)

15 · TIMES REMEMBERED

With the passing of the years, events and actions which in their day might have seemed commonplace take on a patina of antique strangeness and even romance. In settled communities a collective folk-memory is handed down from one generation to the next and brought out at selected moments to satisfy our curiosity about our ancestors. Ghost stories lose nothing in the retelling. Tales of witchcraft and black magic have an indelible quality which preserves their details. Old customs, no longer observed, live on in anecdote.

Here, in the inconsequential way that is natural to them, are some of the recollections that occur to Dorset folk – when the mood takes them.

The Tranters

Such local transport as existed before the days of the motorbus was supplied by the tranters or carriers. The Ashmore carrier's wife has written a most interesting description of their experiences : 'My husband and his father and mother were carriers for over forty years. He himself went to Shaftesbury on Saturdays for twenty-five years. They went to Blandford (by three different roads) three times a week. One day they went by Fontmell, Sutton, Iwerne and Shroton, and when a boy of eleven, my husband used to ride a trace horse to Fontmell to meet the big van to help pull it up the hill. It was often twelve or one o'clock at night before they got home.

Another day they went by Stubhampton, Gunville, Hinton and Pimperne. Often the springs were up very high at Stubhampton. I well remember that in 1910 they were up to the bed of the van, and we had to drive through in a high trap taking orders over the hedges, till we got to Prince's Corner, where the van met us, having been driven round by Larmer Tree. We were met there on our return by another horse which helped to pull the van through the water. It was not a very pleasant experience to hear the water rushing on in the darkness, and the horses stumbling along.

The third day the van went by Bower's Barn along the top road ... Years ago the big van was loaded up with various things from a pair of bootlaces to barrels of beer. Anything and every thing that people wanted, the carriers did their best to bring.'

Dorset Up Along and Down Along

By Word of Mouth

Heard to-day an old country tradition; that if a woman goes off her own premises before being churched, e.g. crosses a road that forms the boundary of her residence – she may be made to do penance or be excommunicated. I cannot explain this, but it reminds me of what old Mr Hibbs of Bere Regis told me lately; that a native of that place, now ninety, says he remembers a young woman doing penance in Bere Church for singing scandalous songs about 'a great lady'. The girl stood in a white sheet while she went through 'the service of penance', whatever that was.

Thomas Hardy (1840-1928)

Lulworth Oysters

At West Lulworth there was an oyster fishery, but the character of this village is rapidly changing. Visitors have come in ever increasing numbers, and pleasure-boats are more profitable than fishing boats.

Since the coming of the Tank Corps camp the area for lobster fishing has been restricted, and the oyster beds which at one time lay around White Nothe, and were very profitable, have disappeared of late years. Old fishermen say that trawlers from the east coast came and dredged up all the fish. The men still bring up quantities of oyster shells from these grounds but, alas, they are always empty. The fishing must have been on a fairly big scale, for a large oyster pond was made on the west of the cove in which the fish were kept until wanted. The outer wall of this pond is still seen at low water. It looks like a row of rocks, and few know its origin.

Dorset Up Along and Down Along, 1935

Marriage Customs

A way of knowing the future husband is to pluck an even ash leaf and, putting it into the hand, to say:

'The even ash leaf in my hand
The first I meet shall be my man.'
Then, putting it into the glove to say:
'The even ash leaf in my glove
The first I meet shall be my love.'
And, lastly, into the bosom, saying:
'The even ash leaf in my bosom
The first I meet shall be my husband.'

Soon after which the future husband will make his appearance, and the lass may observe him as accurately as she will. The scattering of hemp seed was practised by Dorset maidens at Midsummer (i.e., on Old Midsummer's Eve, at midnight) with a like object. A girl would walk through the garden with a rake on her left shoulder and, throwing the hemp seed over her right, would repeat these lines:

'Hemp seed I set, hemp seed I sow,
The man that is my true love come after me and mow,'

when, if the spell worked properly, the future husband should appear behind her with a scythe. . . .

Dorset folk are not peculiar, I believe, in holding the opinion that it is more in consonance with the canons of propriety relating to matters matrimonial that the elder members of a family should marry before the younger ones; but I am not aware that in any other county there is attached any such penance or atonement on the part of the elder ones who permit a breach of this unwritten law as is indicated in the following custom as related to me by an old lady (now dead) in the parish of Symondsbury. If a younger sister or brother of a family were to marry before the elder branches, on the day of the wedding these latter were expected to dance, bare-footed (I believe), over furze bushes placed on the floor. Whether this custom prevailed to any great extent may be questioned, but my informant told me that not so very long before it really did take place, when the parties required satis-factorily underwent their penance of dancing or skipping over the aforesaid "vuzzen."

In connection with the subject of marriage may perhaps be men-tioned the superstition appertaining to the enormous figure cut in the turf on the side of the hill at Cerne Abbas, known as the "Cerne Giant," which has existed there from time immemorial. It is said to be a perfect cure for barren-ness in women if they sit on the actual figure of the giant as cut in the turf; but some say that the married couple desiring issue must actually consummate the marriage on the spot in order to give full effect to the charm.

J.S. Udal (1893)

Witchcraft

Belief in witchcraft dies hard and in many villages memories of particular witches are still vivid. The following stories and traditions speak for themselves:—

'The most notable spot near the village of Leigh is called the Miz-Maze. It is on high ground in an open field, and presents the appear-ance of a slightly raised, flat mound, some paces in diameter. In days too remote for our oldest inhabitants to recall, it was the meeting place of the holiday-makers of Leigh. As late as the year 1800 the Maze existed, in the form of banks made to follow an intricate form. It is a pity that hardly a trace of all this now remains, as the situation is delightful as well as romantic.

In the old days when the practice of witchcraft was fairly general, this spot was a noted gathering place of witches, and as it was remote from a high road or any big town or village, it was not an ill chosen locality for the purpose. Tradition has it that the last witch who was burned in England was arrested when attending a conference in the Miz-Maze at Leigh.' She was burnt at Dorchester, in Maumbury Rings, in the latter half of the seventeenth century.

'Witches abounded until quite recent date at Cheselbourne. One farmer always found a horse in his stable in a terrible sweat in the morning and looking as if he had been ridden fast and far. This was put down to Ol' Ann Riggs, who was held responsible for the death of nine horses in one week – all belonging to this same farmer.'

'One inhabitant of Horton, had, in his boyhood, a relation who was a witch. (Such a family connection is rarely owned). The boy's father used often to complain, on going to the stables, that the horses had been hard-ridden and were covered with foam. He would leave them tied and find them loose. If this witch had a grudge against anyone, that person's cattle or horses would be stricken with malady or lameness.'

The late Mrs. Fudge of Marnhull told the following story : 'As I was standing by my door, (a cottage at the foot of Church Hill) I saw a woman coming down the hill who was a witch or hag. She saw me laugh at her. After I went to bed that night I felt a weight on my legs which gradually went upwards to my chest. I screamed, and my son came into the room. As he opened the door, the lump fell off, and I distinctly heard the hag walk down the stairs and out of the door.' This is an instance of a belief which used to be widely held in the west.

Dorset Up Along and Down Along, 1935

Chimney Smoking

At Shipton one day, 'while a chimney sweep was engaged at work, he brought from a chimney a bullock's heart, stuffed with pins, the strangest thing being, not that the heart should ever get up a chimney at all, but that the pins were all stuck in the wrong way, that is, they were pointing outward, like the prickles of a hedgehog.'

Again in 1930, Mrs. Carlton of Winterbourne Kingston writes: 'The architect who planned the alteration of this house told me there were hundreds of bottles hidden in chimneys in Dorset. This has also been corroborated by our ancient chimney-sweep. In a farm-house in the neighbourhood a bottle was found hanging by a wire up in the old chimney, and, when it was cut down, was found to contain liquid. It was tightly corked and the cork stuck all over with pins. After the bottle was broken and the liquid spilled the family had nothing but bad luck and finally left the place. The bottle is supposed to prevent bad spirits entering the house.'

The heart stuck with pins, points outwards, was considered to be efficacious in the same way. At Wyke Regis they had various traditions, 'there was an old woman who used to smoke a clay pipe and was supposed to be a witch. A young woman had her arm rendered useless by her, and a gipsy woman coming to the house, told the girl's mother to take a bullock's heart and stick a hundred pins into it and hang it in the chimney. When the heart dried up it fell down and was burnt and the old woman was seen tearing her hair in a rage and saying that someone had been meddling with her affairs.'

Dorset Up Along and Down Along, 1935

Mr Warry says that a farmer who was a tenant of a friend of his used to take the heart of every calf that died, and, sticking it full of black thorns, hang it on the cotterel, or cross-bar, of his chimney: this was done to prevent the spread of the disease that had killed the calf. When the next tenant came the chimney smoked very much, and examining it, they found it choked with hearts treated in the manner described – by that time dry and parched.

Thomas Hardy (1840-1928)

The Toad Doctor

'Somewhere between 1830 and 1840 a Toad Doctor lived at Pulham near Cerne. His name was Buckland and every year in the month of May, according to the phase of the moon, Dr. Buckland's Fair was held. The doctor, dressed in white, was assisted by his three daughters, also dressed in white, and they attended the patients who came from far and near. His method was certainly unusual, for he kept toads which he used alive, hanging them under his patient's clothes. As long as the toads twitched and moved, the cure progressed! As to what happened if the toad died before the cure was complete the story does not relate.'

News of this Toad Doctor also comes from Sturminster Newton. It is said that many of the people who visited him were suffering from the effects of 'overlooking' by those who had the Evil Eye.

Dorset Up Along and Down Along, 1935

An old man, a wizard, used to bring toads' legs in little bags to Bagber Bridge, where he was met by crowds of people who came in vehicles and on foot, and bought them as charms to cure scrofula by wearing them round the neck. These legs were supposed to twitch occasionally in the bag, and probably did, when it gave the wearer's blood a 'turn,' and changed the course of the disease.

Thomas Hardy (1840-1928)

Three Good Neighbours

He that hath a good warreyne of Conies, a good dovehouse, and good fishepondes, shall need the lesse to go into the Forest or Chase for beefe or bacon, for these three are good neighbours.

George Turbervile (The Noble Arte of Venerie, 1576)

The Candle Auction

A custom ran in Moonfleet when either land or lease was put up to bidding, to stick a pin in a candle; and so long as the pin held firm, it was open to any to make a better offer, but when the flame burnt down and the pin fell out, then land or lease fell to the last bidder.

John Meade Falkner (Moonfleet, 1898)

A 'Skimmity' at West Stour

This village has been, on several evenings recently, the scene of some very disgraceful demonstrations. A crowd of men, women and children have made night hideous with screams, shouts, the rattling of old tin vessels, and the parading of effigies through the streets. The disturbances were brought to a close with the burning of the figures of the obnoxious parties. Wife-beating, especially when indulged in by one who, from his position in the parish, ought to be an example to others, is disgraceful and indefensible, but every sensible person must deprecate such a barbarous mode of censuring the crime as that which is resorted to in rural districts.

Western Gazette, 10 October 1869

16 · SURPRISES, LEGENDS AND MARVELS

At its conclusion a bedside book should drift into dreams and fantasies and those oddities which give life its stranger colours. But no nightmares.

Sleep well.

The High Sheriff and the Wooden Leg

When a prisoner is sentenced to death the High Sheriff has either to hang the man himself or else stand the hang-man's expenses. These come to not less than £35 and in return the dead man's clothes and other belongings become the perquisites of the High Sheriff.

When Wilfrid Brymer was High Sheriff, he had to hang a man with a wooden leg. One of his tenants, who kept a public house, asked Brymer to give him the wooden leg. This Brymer did and it was exhibited in the bar parlour. Not long after, Brymer received a bill for the leg, for it appeared that the man had never paid for it; and as it had become the property of the High Sheriff, the firm which supplied the leg requested Brymer to pay for it, which he had to do.

Unpublished memoirs of Edward Castleman (1870-1946)

An Unusual Epitaph

*In the graveyard at St John's, Charlton (near Shaftesbury) the
headstone of Herbert William Bryans (1856-1925) – youngest son of a
youngest son – bears his own brief chronicle of the days of his life:*

For ten years I made tea in India
For two I made wine in France
For thirty stained glass windows in England
And bad puns all the time.

The Cerne Giant

It has been reported to have been made by Lord Holles's servants,
during his residence here: but it is more likely he only caused it to be
repaired; for some people who died not long since, 80 or 90 years old,
when young knew some of the same age, that averred it was there
beyond the memory of man. There is a tradition, that a giant, who
resided hereabout in former ages, the pest and terror of the adjacent
country, having made an excursion into Blackmore, and regaled himself with several sheep, retired to this hill, and lay down to sleep. The
country people seized this opportunity, pinioned him down, and killed
him, and then traced out the dimensions of his body, to perpetuate his
memory.

Fabulous as this story is, it is perhaps a proof of the great antiquity
of this figure. It extends over near an acre of ground, as does the White
Horse in Berkshire, which is 150 feet from the head to the withers. It
seems to have been executed by persons who were not quite unac-
quainted with the rules of proportion observed by statuaries and
painters, who anciently allowed seven or eight hands to the length of a
human body. It is repaired about once in seven years, by the people of
the town, by cleansing the furrows, and filling them with fresh chalk.
Scouring the White Horse is a custom, and festival solemnized from
time immemorial, by a numerous concourse of people from the adjacent villages. If there ever was any particular day in the year for
this purpose here, the memory of it is now lost, and the operation

performed just when the towns-people think fit. Most antiquaries
agree that it is a monument of high antiquity, and make little doubt
but that it was a representation of the Saxon god Heil; so that it must
be more ancient at least than AD 600, soon after which time the
Saxons were converted to Christianity.

The late learned Mr Wise, who from an excess of delicacy declined
to illustrate this singular monument, supposes it of much later date
than the two figures of White Horses in Berkshire and Wiltshire which
he refers to the Saxon Times.

John Hutchins (1774)

Poole: A Bloody Shower

In 1653, a phenomenon was observed in this place: a black cloud hung
over it for about two hours, and at last burst, but instead of common
waters, the whole was like a shower of blood, which dyed whatever
substance it fell upon of a deep scarlet colour.

James Dugdale (The New British Traveller, 1819)

Batcombe: a Legend

To those in search of out-of-the-way places where may be found the
quiet of the boundless prairie I would commend Batcombe. Its situation at the foot of a curving line of steep chalk downs is most romantic;
its approach from the South by a headlong road which drops over the
green cliff is most fearsome. The village has long vanished, having fled
apparently to escape the boredom of unutterable solitude, leaving behind a church, a farmhouse, and a few cottages. The church stands
quite alone at the bottom of the silent downs, which surround it on
three sides. So steep are these grass-covered heights that from their
summit it is possible to look down upon the flat roof of the tower. The
church possesses a font of most archaic design, and many monuments
which are evidently the work of village stone-masons who had vivid
fancies in their brains.

On the embattled tower are four pinnacles, one at each corner. Until
a few years ago there were only three. The fourth was knocked off by
the hoof of the squire's horse when that gentleman jumped from the
crest of the down into the village, clearing the church and tower on his

way. The squire, whose name was John Minterne, was better known as 'Conjuring Minterne'. He had dealings with the devil, so the story goes, and the extraordinary feats he performed by the aid of this being must have kept the villagers in a state of chronic uneasiness. Possibly the uncanny habits of the squire led to the depopulation of the settlement. It is to be regretted that *The Life and Times of Conjuring Minterne* has not yet been written. Certain it is that he ceased to associate with the devil before he died, for he is buried in the churchyard, in holy ground. His tomb is pointed out with pride to any who turn aside to visit this quaint place. It is small and square and singularly carved, but lacks both name and date, as well as any record of the life work of this alarming man.

Sir Frederick Treves (1906)

The Gappergennies of Ashmore

There was a barrow, over which the road to Fontmell now runs, by Folly Hanging Gate, near Washers Pit. In this lonely place, till within living memory, strange sounds were made by creatures in the air called Gapper-gennies. Of the nature of these sounds I have not been able to learn anything, except that they could be successfully imitated by human lips. When, perhaps fifty years ago, a metallic road was made to Fontmell instead of the old cart-track, this barrow was dug up, and the bones it contained buried in the churchyard. On the down, by the roadside, a cross had always been kept cut, opposite the barrow. This has been neglected since the reinterment; and since then, also, the strange sounds have not been heard. The low mound and the cross on the turf are well remembered.

E.W. Watson (Ashmore, 1890)

Blue Vinny

When I moved down to Wessex a new delight entered my life: Blue Vinny. It is my staple midday fodder. It is paradisal. I heap this divine cheese in moist mounds upon Bath Olivers, and consume it with raw onion and a glass of red plonk.

Its aromatic richness seeps through one's veins. There is an afterglow lasting hours. The hairs on one's wrists are springier.

In an 1888 glossary of our dialect which I have 'vinny' is given as 'mouldy or mildewy from damp or fungus; blue mouldy cheese'. I suppose it can be reduced to that brutal analysis. At its finest it is, I swear, nobler than Stilton.

It does vary. It can be dry and dusty – then it's called 'chock-dog'. Or it can sometimes be a bit 'bulky', or sharp on the tongue. I'm told that it is vital that each individual cheese is made from the milk of one individual cow, and that must be a beast of singular merit. A factory tried turning it out. It failed. This subtlety is beyond machine mass production.

Of course the character of a local skim milk cheese depends not only upon inherited knowledge of when to drain the whey and salt the curd layers, but upon soil and pasture and climate.

Once there were scores of local varieties of cheese made, throughout Britain with flavours and textures peculiar to each region, and doubtless many were pretty chewy, coarse fodder for medieval palates. But why did Shropshire cheese vanish? Why did Kent and Essex lose the knack which once placed the county names like coronets on their product? Surely, Banbury should not have decided to put all its energy into cake-making and allowed the cheese of that sobriquet to become obsolete?

Still, I am consoled by the unique smatch of Blue Vinny.

Wild garlic grows thick down here. The white flower stars appropriately stink to high heaven. If a herd gets among garlic, next day's milk is tipped down the drain. It gives a tang to the cornflakes and tea people don't fancy. My theory is that this pungency seeps through into the cheese.

It is likely that you have never tasted Blue Vinny. I made enquiries in London; Fortnum's don't stock it; Harrods once did but can no longer get it; Selfridges don't have it.

Paxton and Whitfield, in Jermyn Street, obtain some now and then, but know of only two sources. 'And,' said the manageress, 'they guard the secret so closely that they won't pass it on. It's a dying cheese.'

I was filled with dread. Even here, in the ancient motherlode, it is like striking a seam of gold. When I was originally trying to sniff it out, an empty-handed grocer sighed: 'There was a young woman near Emminster who made lovely Vinny, but she married and moved. There's somewhere at Sherton Abbas you can still get it – if you know the right approach.'

You see in what a ticklish day-to-day state of tension the Vinny addict lives. I eventually discovered a small dairy where the sublime cylinders fragrantly moulder. Even the serving girls don't know where they come from, only that they are delivered by someone from Ivell.

He is merely a go-between, a front man. I often think of an anonymous van scurrying under cover of darkness through our twisting lanes, priceless cargo cloaked by an old tarpaulin, the driver's eyes alert beneath hat brim for lurking cheesejackers.

But I have no scruples where Blue Vinny is concerned. Like Chicago's citizens during Prohibition, as long as I get my supply of the real stuff I ask no questions.

Kenneth Allsop (In the Country, 1972)

LIST OF SOURCES

Textual sources are listed below alphabetically by author's name and indicate the title and date of the edition consulted, which is not necessarily the earliest published version. In the main text the date given with the author's name is either the date of first publication or, when appropriate, the dates of the author's birth and death.

In some cases I have been obliged to abridge, and occasionally to sub-edit minimally, in order to settle an extract comfortably in its new surroundings – but with a care that I hope their authors might approve or would forgive.

Allingham, William : *William Allingham: a Diary*. Macmillan 1907
Allsop, Kenneth: *In the Country*. Hamish Hamilton 1972
Aubrey, John (1626-1696): *Natural History of Wiltshire*. David and Charles 1969
Austen, Jane: *Persuasion*
Bankes, George: *The Story of Corfe Castle*. 1853
Banks, Sir Joseph: *Journal 1767*. Dorset Nat Hist & Arch Soc Proceedings XXI, 1899
Barnes, William: *One Hundred Poems*. Dorset Bookshop, Blandford 1971
Beckford, Peter: *Thoughts on Hunting 1781*
Beerbohm, Max: *Max in Verse*. Heinemann. Stephen Greene Press
Belloc, Hilaire: *The Cruise of the Nona*. London 1925. Penguin 1958
Betjeman, John: *First and Last Loves*. Murray 1952
  Collected Poems. Murray 1970
Brooke, Rupert: *Collected Poems*, ed. E. Marsh (with memoir)
Burney, Fanny: *Diary and Letters of Mme. D'Arblay 1904*
Byng, John (Viscount Torrington): *The Torrington Diaries*. Eyre & Spottiswoode 1934
Castleman, Edward (1870-1946): Unpublished Memoirs
Cecil, Lord David: *Some Dorset Country Houses*. Dovecote Press 1985
Chafin, William: *Anecodotes of Cranborne Chase 1818*
Coker: *See Gerard*

Cooper, Anthony Ashley (1st Earl of Shaftesbury): 'A Fragment of Autobiography' in A Life of Anthony Ashley Cooper, first Earl of Shaftesbury: W. D. Christie. Macmillan 1871

Crowe, William: Lewesdon Hill. John Murray 1827

Drayton, Michael: Poly-olbion 1622

Dugdale, James: The New British Traveller 1819

Falkner, John Meade: Moonfleet 1898

Fiennes, Celia: The Journeys of, ed. Christopher Morris. Cresset Press 1947

Forster, E. M: T. E. Lawrence by his Friends. A. W. Lawrence. Cape 1937

Foster, J. J: Wessex Worthies. Dicksons 1920

Fowles, John: The French Lieutenant's Woman. Cape 1969

Frampton, Mary: Journal of Mary Frampton. ed. H. G. Mundy. Sampson Low 1885

Fuller, Thomas: History of the Worthies of England 1662

Gasquest, Francis Aidan: The Great Pestilence 1893

Gerard, Thomas: Coker's Survey of Dorsetshire

Ham, Elizabeth: Elizabeth Ham by herself, ed. Eric Gillett. Faber 1945

Hardy, Thomas: The Life of Thomas Hardy. Macmillan 1972

   The Complete Poems, ed. James Gibson. Macmillan 1976

   'The Dorsetshire Labourer' 1883 in Hardy, Stories & Poems ed. Donald J. Morrison. Everyman's Library. Dent 1970

   Personal Notebooks, ed. Richard H. Taylor 1978

   The Novels: Desperate Remedies, The Return of the Native, Tess of the D'Urbervilles

Hudson, W.H: Birds and Man 1915

Hutchings, Monica: Inside Dorset. Abbey Press, Sherborne 1965

Hutchins, John: History and Antiquities of Dorset

Hyland, Paul: Purbeck. Gollancz 1978

Lang, W. D: Mary Anning. 'Natural History Magazine'. n.d.

Lawrence, T. E. Letter to Robert Graves. Letters of T. E. Lawrence. Cape 1938

Leland, John: Itinerary of, ed. Lucy Toulmin Smith. Bell 1907

Loudon, John Claudius: In Search of English Gardens. Century 1990

Loveless, George: Victims of Whiggery. London 1837

Massingham, H. J: The English Downland. Batsford 1936

Morley, Geoffrey: Smuggling in Hampshire & Dorset 1700-1850.

Countryside Books 1983

Morton, H. V: *In Search of England*

Moule, H. J: *Old Dorset*. Cassell 1893

North, Roger: *The Lives of the Norths*. 1890

Pinney, Azariah: *The Pinney Papers*

Pococke, Richard: *Travels through England* 1754 ed. J. J. Cartwright
    1888-89

Powys, Llewelyn: *Dorset Essays* 1935 (Bodley Head).
    Thirteen Worthies 1924

Roberts, George: *History and Antiquities of Lyme Regis*. 1834

Sansom, Clive: *Dorset Village*. Methuen 1962

Scott, Sir Walter: Inscription in a copy of William Chafin's *Anecdotes*
    1818

Shaftesbury, First Earl of: see Cooper, Ashley

Smeaton, John: *History of the Eddystone Lighthouse*. (cited John
    Hutchins: *History of Dorset*)

Smith, R. Bosworth: *Bird Life and Bird Lore*. John Murray

Stanley of Alderley, Lady (in a letter): *The Ladies of Alderley*. Hamish
    Hamilton 1938

Street, Sean: *This True Making*. KQBX Press 1992

Surtees, R. S: *New Sporting Magazine*

Treves, Frederick: *Highways and Byways in Dorset*. Macmillan 1906

Turbervile, George: *The Noble Art of Venerie* 1576

Udal, J. S: *Marriage Customs*. Dorset Nat. Hist. and Arch. Proc.1893

Warner, Richard: *Literary Recollections* 1830

Watson, E. W: *Ashmore* 1890

Wesley, John: *Journal of*, ed. Nora Ratcliff. Nelson 1940

Wheeler, Sir Mortimer: General Augustus Pitt-Rivers. BBC Radio 'The
    Old General' 1953

Wightman, Ralph: *The Wessex Heathland*. Hale 1953
    My Homeward Road 1950
    'The Springs of Blackmore Vale.' BBC Radio 1944

Williams, Alfred: *Life in a Railway Factory*. Alan Sutton 1984

Wilson, Harriette: *Memoirs*, 1825. Reprinted as *Mistress of Many*. ed.
    Max Marquis, Paul Elek 1960

Women's Institutes [symposium]: *Dorset Up Along and Down Along*

Wymer, Norman: *A Breath of England*. Batsford 1948

Wynne, Eugenia: *The Wynne Diaries*. O.U.P. 1940

ACKNOWLEDGEMENTS

I am grateful to the following for allowing the inclusion of both prose and poetry which remains in copyright: Michael Joseph Publishing for Kenneth Allsop's account of Blue Vinny cheese in *In the Country*; John Murray (Publishers) Ltd for an extract from *First and Last Loves* and 'Dorset' from *Collected Poems* by John Betjeman; Jonathan Cape for the opening paragraphs of *The French Lieutenant's Woman* by John Fowles; Shelleys the Printers (the Abbey Press) for *Inside Dorset* by Monica Hutchings; Paul Hyland for two extracts from *Purbeck, The Ingrained Island*; B. T. Batsford Ltd for *The English Downland* by H. J. Massingham; Countryside Books for a piece from *Smuggling in Hampshire and Dorset* by Geoffrey Morley; Methuen & Co Ltd for the verses from Clive Sansom's *Dorset Village*; the KQBX Press for 'Poole Quay' by Sean Street from *This True Making*; the Estate of Ralph Wightman for extracts from *My Homeward Road* and *The Wessex Heathland*.

The engravings that decorate the chapter headings are taken from *Dorset Up Along and Down Along* (1935); *Wood Engravings of Thomas Bewick* (1953); *Shaftesbury* (1932) by John. R. Biggs and James. E. Masters; *Anecdotes and History of Cranborne Chase* (1818) by William Chafin; *Unknown Dorset* (1927) by Donald Maxwell; *The Royal Warren, or Picturesque Rambles in the Isle of Purbeck* (1882) by C. E. Robinson; *The History of Dorchester, during the British, Roman, Saxon and Norman Periods* (1833) by J. Savage; and *The Buildings of Old Portland* (1979) by Eric Ricketts, to whom I am particularly indebted for allowing the use of his drawing of a traction engine hauling stone at Weston.